AWESOME MINDS

COMIC BOOK CREATORS

Library of Congress Cataloging-in-Publication Data available upon request.
ISBN: 978-1-947458-77-2

duopress books are available at special discounts when purchased in bulk for sales promotions as well as for fund-raising or educational use. Special editions can be created to specification. Contact us at hello@duopressbooks.com for more information.

This book is an independent, unauthorized, and unofficial biography and account of the people involved in the development and history of comic books and is not endorsed or sponsored by Archie Comic Publications, Inc.; Comic Market (popularly known as Comiket); Dark Horse Comics; DC Comics, Inc. (part of DC Entertainment, Inc., subsidiary of Warner Bros. Entertainment Inc., subsidiary of Warner Media, LLC, subsidiary of AT&T Inc.); Dell Publishing; Drawn & Quarterly; E. C. Publications, Inc.; Fantagraphics Books; Festival International de la Bande Dessinée (known in English as Angoulême International Comics Festival); Finnair (part of Finnair Group); Fuji Television Network, Inc. (part of Fuji Media Holdings, Inc.); Hachette (part of Lagardère Publishing); Hearst Communications, Inc.; *La Prensa* (part of Multimedios La Capital); Lucca Comics and Games (organized by Comune di Lucca); Marvel Comics (part of Marvel Entertainment, LLC, subsidiary of the Walt Disney Company); Mushi Productions; Nippon Animation Co., Ltd.; the Procter & Gamble Company; San Diego Comic-Con International; Shogakukan, Inc. (part of Hitotsubashi Group); Skorpio; Societé Dargaud; Tezuka Productions Co., Ltd.; Toei Animation Co., Ltd. (part of Toei Company, Ltd., TV Asahi Holdings Corporation—owned by the Asahi Shimbun Company, Toei Co., Ltd, Mizuho Trust & Banking through Trust & Custody Services Bank, Kyushu Asahi Broadcasting, Recruit, State Street BTC of Japan, the Asahi Shimbun Foundation, Northern Trust, and the Master Trust Bank of Japan—Bandai Namco Holdings, Inc., Fuji Media Holdings, Inc., and Sony Corporation); Valiant Comics (part of DMG Entertainment); Viacom, Inc.; WaRP Graphics; *Weekly Young Magazine* (*Shukan Yangu Magajin*, in Japanese, published by Kodansha Ltd.); Will Eisner Comic Industry Awards; or any other person or entity owning or controlling rights in their name, trademark, or copyrights.

Trademarks, trade names, and characters depicted and referred to herein are the property of the respective owners and are used solely to identify the particular comic book or work with which such trademark, trade name, or character is associated.

Manufactured in China
10 9 8 7 6 5 4 3 2 1
Duo Press LLC
8 Market Place, Suite 300
Baltimore, MD 21202
Distributed by Workman Publishing Company, Inc.

Published simultaneously in Canada by Thomas Allen & Son Limited.
To order: hello@duopressbooks.com
www.workman.com
www.duopressbooks.com

AWESOME MINDS

COMIC BOOK CREATORS

BY
ALEJANDRO ARBONA

ART BY
CHELSEA O'MARA HOLEMAN

duopress

We asked the author:

Who is your comic book creator hero?

Without a doubt, Steve Ditko; even though I can't say I agree with his philosophy or his politics…the inventiveness and the sheer, wonderful weirdness of what Ditko created—Spider-Man, Doctor Strange, their bad guys, and countless chilling tales of sci-fi and horror—had no match even among fellow geniuses of his time like Jack Kirby and Will Eisner.

—Alejandro Arbona

Now, we ask you:

Who is your comic book creator hero?

CONTENTS

INTRODUCTION

COMICS, COMIC BOOKS, COMIC STRIPS, GRAPHIC NOVELS... the first riddle we run into when we talk about comics is figuring out the difference between these terms.

The origin of modern comics is recent in our history; comics as we know them today have existed for only a little over a hundred years. In that short time, they've grown from a disposable form of entertainment—printed on cheap paper and destined for the garbage—to a massive creative engine powering billion-dollar Hollywood movies. But until recently, the medium of comics was considered so juvenile and unsophisticated that there wasn't much study or discussion of the art form for a long time. As a result, a vocabulary never developed for talking about comics; there isn't clarity in what different terms mean. Similar words refer to different things, and very different words describe the same things.

When we talk about comic books, comic strips, and graphic novels, the main difference is in the format of the story. Comic books are short installments of an ongoing story (often serialized issues in a continuing series), released in the form of floppy magazines held together with staples or in thin bound books that in Europe are called "albums." Comic strips are very short stories you see daily or weekly in newspapers and magazines, or online, as webcomics. A bound, book-length, standalone story, with a beginning and an end, designed to sit on a bookshelf with the title printed on the spine is what people call a graphic novel. No matter the packaging, these all contain the same medium of art and entertainment: comics.

As a concept, "comics" is hard to define, but usually, you know them when you see them: stories told through drawings in sequence, in which time passes from panel to panel, with or without text for dialogue and narration. Does a one-panel illustrated gag with a caption underneath count? That's called a "cartoon" (not to be confused with animated cartoons you see on television or online…here's this problem with limited

Picture book

Once upon a time there was a little house in the woods.

A very special little girl lived in the little house in the woods.

Sequential art

vocabulary again). Is a picture book for little kids considered a graphic novel? No, because those stories are told in writing, with one drawing per page illustrating what the text describes. The difference is subtle, but picture books tell a story through language, only complemented by the art. Telling a story through sequential art primarily, with or without text—that's comics.

Humans have been illustrating stories for as long as we've existed. Prehistoric cave paintings, Egyptian hieroglyphs, Japanese illustrated scrolls, the 11th-century Bayeux Tapestry in France, and Mexico's 14th-century manuscript about the early Oaxacan ruler Eight Deer Jaguar Claw are all versions of sequential art stories—comics! In the 19th century, the Swiss cartoonist Rodolphe Töpffer drew his own picture stories, distributing them to bookstores and printing them in magazines; he effectively invented comic books. However, the mass-produced medium we know today is only as old as the modern newspaper. In the late 1890s, one-panel newspaper cartoons of political and social satire began to evolve into multi-panel comic strips…notably *Hogan's Alley* by Richard F. Outcault, featuring the world's first comics character, the Yellow Kid. Other early innovative comic strips like Winsor McCay's *Little Nemo in Slumberland* and Bud Fisher's *Mutt & Jeff* helped this newborn art form evolve.

The Yellow Kid, by Richard F. Outcault

There are enough comic strip cartoonists and graphic novelists to fill several books about their fascinating lives…but we'll stick to comic books after they split off in their evolution from newspaper strips. These are just a few of the artists who created innovative, influential comic books in floppy magazine and album format all around the world.

CHAPTER 1

MAXWELL AND
WILLIAM GAINES

THIS FATHER-AND-SON PUBLISHING DUO
OVERSAW THE ORIGIN STORY OF
THE COMIC BOOK AND THE FIASCO THAT
NEARLY BROUGHT COMIC BOOKS
TO AN END.

Newspaper comics swelled in popularity during the first few decades of the 20th century. By the early 1930s, dozens of printing presses all across the U.S. were cranking out "the funny pages." Eastern Color Printing, based in Connecticut, printed the funnies for papers in New York and New England…but their focus would change in 1933 with the arrival of an ambitious new salesperson.

Maxwell Gaines

Maxwell Gaines (born Ginzberg) had been a schoolteacher and principal who believed in the power of funny talking animals to deliver messages of moral instruction. He joined Eastern Color in 1933, where he had the idea to pitch comic strips to companies with products to advertise. Partnering with newspaper comics publishers to reprint their strips, Eastern Color produced *Funnies on Parade* in 1933, an eight-page giveaway that customers could send for with coupons from Procter & Gamble products.

On the strength of this and other giveaways, Gaines made a deal with Dell Publishing the same year to collect Dell's strips in a full-color floppy magazine and sell it. They called it *Famous Funnies: A Carnival of Comics*. The following year, in 1934, Eastern Color launched *Famous Funnies* as an ongoing monthly series that ran for over 200 issues. This was widely considered the world's first comic book.

Famous Funnies consisted of reruns, but the huge success of this innovative comic book inspired Malcolm Wheeler-Nicholson—a World War I veteran and writer of adventure stories in pulp magazines—to start a company and publish original comics. Wheeler-Nicholson called his comic book *More Fun Comics,* and his company was called National Allied Publications. (The paths of Gaines and Wheeler-Nicholson would cross again soon.) The comic book was now born.

Max Gaines became the director of a new company. Published entertainment was big business in the 1930s—newspapers, magazines, pulpy paperback novels, and now comic books were as lucrative as Hollywood productions—and companies sprang up to cash in. When Malcolm Wheeler-Nicholson left National Allied Publications in 1938, the new CEO, Harry Donenfeld, gave Gaines financing, and together they founded All-American Publications—the birthplace of Wonder Woman, Green Lantern, and the Flash. But Gaines thought he saw the superhero fad ending, and he wanted to publish a different kind of comic book. He eventually let his partners take over All-American, keeping only his favorite comic: *Picture Stories from the Bible.*

National Allied Publications (the home of Superman) and All-American Publications (Wonder Woman) merged with a third Wheeler-Nicholson/Donenfeld company, Detective Comics (where Batman was born), to become DC Comics. With his *Picture Stories from the Bible*, Gaines started a publishing company of his own in 1944 called Educational Comics.

William Gaines—Max's 25-year-old son—planned to become a science teacher. But when his

William Gaines

father died in 1947 at the age of 52 in a boating accident, Bill inherited EC Comics. Needless to say, Bill's vision was different than his old man's. With the company a hundred thousand dollars in debt, the younger Gaines canceled the religious tracts and funny animal comics, started publishing thrilling and salacious material full of violence and horror, and rebranded the entire operation. Educational Comics became Entertaining Comics.

Through the 1940s and early 1950s, the American comic book industry was a major force in kids' entertainment and popular culture. It was called the Golden Age, when Superman, Batman, Wonder Woman, Captain America, and more debuted. They weren't reaching other shores in huge quantities just yet, but in the U.S., millions of kids read comic books every week. And it wasn't only superheroes; the total output of American comic books was split between stories of war, science fiction, cops vs. gangsters, horror, humor, and more. These comics were wild and lawless, packed to the gutters with inky renditions of violence and all manner of moral decay. Virtually every kid in America read them…and the man publishing the very best, most gruesome, smartest, funniest, best-drawn comics in all those genres—*Tales from the Crypt*, *Vault of Horror*, *Two-Fisted Tales*, *Frontline Combat*, *Crime SuspenStories*, *Weird Science*, *Mad*, and more—was Bill Gaines.

Sooner or later, the raucous party had to end. A psychiatrist named Fredric Wertham observed some of his troubled young patients and began to suspect that comic books were inspiring young readers to become violent thugs and juvenile delinquents. Even though Dr. Wertham was an intelligent and compassionate man who had championed racial equality and progressive causes, his 1954 book *Seduction of the Innocent* was intolerant and homophobic, in addition to shortsighted. Wertham found that all of his violent patients had grown up reading comics, so he believed comics caused their behavior. But practically every American child read comics at the time, including ones who went to church dutifully and got straight A's in school.

Spurred by Wertham's book, the U.S. government formed the Senate Subcommittee on Juvenile Delinquency to shake down entertainment industries believed to cause teen violence. Among the people called to testify in 1954, Bill Gaines made the biggest—and most unfortunate—splash. He had been taking diet pills, which in the '50s contained amphetamines and were highly addictive. On the day of his testimony, crashing from amphetamine withdrawal, Gaines let the senators score points on him,

defending the good taste of a comic book featuring a woman's severed head on the cover—*Crime SuspenStories* #22. Gaines's testimony benefited the subcommittee's side more than his.

These hearings didn't lead to official repercussions, but comic book companies were so embarrassed, and so fearful of government reprisal, that they elected to censor themselves. Publishers agreed to abide by the rules of their own Comics Code Authority, which barred comics from depicting sex, violence, or questionable morals. Under the Comics Code, themes of the occult, the undead, and anything that undermined Christian values were banned. Bad guys couldn't win, and good had to triumph, usually with a heavy-handed ethical lesson at the end. Quality suffered; many writers and artists lost work and never created comics again. Sales plummeted, and the industry nearly collapsed.

Of all the publishers, Gaines was hit the hardest. The limitations of the Comics Code ended EC's crime and horror lines. To escape the shackles of censorship, Gaines turned one of his best sellers, *Mad,* into a magazine, not subject to the Comics Code.

Many of EC's finest comic books are now collected in handsome archival editions. Bill Gaines died in 1992 at the age of 70. He is best remembered as the jolly, bearded face of *Mad Magazine*, the sole vestige of his legacy still being published today.

CHAPTER 2

JERRY SIEGEL
AND JOE SHUSTER

IN THE YEARS BEFORE WORLD WAR II, TWO
KIDS GROWING UP IN CLEVELAND, OHIO, BECAME
FRIENDS OVER THEIR LOVE OF SCIENCE FICTION
AND WENT TO WORK WRITING AND DRAWING THEIR
OWN COMIC STRIPS. THE CHARACTER THEY
CREATED—SUPERMAN—CHANGED THE WORLD.

The year 1938 was a time of upheaval. The United States had always welcomed immigrants from all over the world; suddenly, during the 1930s, America's borders were seeing a steady increase of Jewish refugees from Germany, Austria, Poland, and surrounding countries.

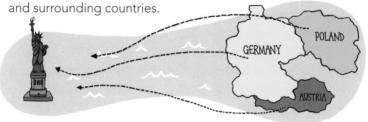

In Europe, those countries were the center of disastrous transformation. For nearly twenty years in Germany, the National Socialist German Workers' Party—the Nazi Party—had been on the rise in politics. During the 1930s, as the forces of Adolf Hitler seized power in the German government, newly formed police and military units began to target Jewish citizens, as well as people who were black, gay, or transgender, or anyone the Nazis deemed undesirable. Jews and others were being victimized, arrested, put in concentration camps, and killed. By 1938, Nazi control of Germany was complete; in 1939, their tyranny spread beyond German borders when Hitler invaded Poland, starting a war across Europe, then the world. Some people were able to foresee bad things coming; they left their homes and their country before things got too deadly. Others managed to escape during the worst of it, fleeing to the U.S. and other safe nations. But millions didn't make it; during the mass extermination of the Holocaust, six million Jews died in Europe.

This chilling history helps explain some of the symbolic appeal of the world's first superhero in 1938: the only survivor of a dying planet, sent away as a baby in a last-ditch hope to save his life, comes to Earth with powers and abilities far beyond those of mortal men. This was Superman, created by two young Jewish men in Cleveland, Ohio.

Jerry Siegel was the writer; Joe Shuster, the artist. Both were born in 1914—Jerry in Cleveland, Joe in Toronto, Canada—and both were living in Cleveland when they met at age 16 in high school. They were the children of immigrants; Jerry's parents came from Lithuania, while Joe's father was from the Netherlands and his mother was from Ukraine. As science fiction fans, they became fast friends. Jerry had started his own homemade magazine of stories, simply titled *Science Fiction*. Cultural historians consider it the first known "fanzine," a fan-made magazine.

In the third issue of *Science Fiction*, in 1933, Siegel and Shuster ran a comic called "The Reign of the Super-Man"; ironically, this wasn't the birth of their legendary hero but the story of a bald-headed villain with mental powers. They were never able to sell the idea to a publisher. Siegel and Shuster reimagined a different character to suit the name, a hero. They created a six-page story titled *The Superman* and peddled it to every comic book company in the phone book.

Even the revised strip—about a Superman with no costume, given powers against his will by a scientist—was of no interest to publishers, and Shuster destroyed the pages; only a couple of those early drawings survived. Siegel tried new versions of the Superman idea with different artists, never with any luck. In one version, Superman was a scientist from the future who came back in a time machine; in another, inching closer to the final concept, Superman was sent back in time by his parents to save their child from Earth's imminent destruction.

Meanwhile, Siegel and Shuster continued to develop new characters and strips together. By 1935, they found a little work with Malcolm Wheeler-Nicholson and his new publisher, National Allied Publications, in the landmark *More Fun Comics*. Publishing a few adventure comics gave Siegel and Shuster a chance to pitch more. They returned to their Superman concept, fleshing out his backstory and abilities, inspired by the science fiction that nourished their imagination.

Malcolm Wheeler-Nicholson

Stories of spaceships and aliens gave them dreams of an exploding planet and a rocket that crashes to Earth. Reading the novel *Gladiator* by Philip Wylie, they were inspired by a bulletproof man with incredible strength who could leap great distances. Surrounded by economic hardship during the Great Depression, they dreamed of a kind-hearted hero with the strength to fight corrupt politicians, racketeering criminals, and abusers of all sorts, even a man who beats his wife—all three the kinds of bad guys Superman clobbered in his very first adventure.

What happened next has been a cautionary lesson for aspiring creators ever since. Jerry Siegel and Joe Shuster sold the first Superman story to National Allied Publications— giving away all rights of ownership of the character and any future profits—at $10 a page. For the 13-page story, they were paid $130 to split between them. After years of struggle, it must have seemed like a tremendous sum, like they'd finally hit it big; they also had no way to know just how successful Superman would become. But this was more than just a one-off comic book story; in Superman, Siegel and Shuster created the world's first superhero, with all the trappings of a costume, powers, and a secret identity—that of Clark Kent, a mild-mannered newspaper reporter. Superman inspired imitators, but more importantly, he opened the flood-gates for an entirely new genre: the superhero comic book.

National Allied Publications—and the company it went on to become, DC Comics—made a fortune from Superman comics, merchandise, movies, TV shows, video games, and more.

Jerry Siegel and Joe Shuster wrote and drew Superman comics for DC, and they earned a good paycheck for it, but nowhere near the wealth they deserved. In the following decades, any time their contracts came up for renewal or rights were set to expire, Siegel and Shuster sued the publisher to reclaim a share of their creation, but they were unsuccessful. In 1975, the comic book artists Jerry Robinson and Neal Adams joined the fight, lobbying to restore Siegel and Shuster's creator credits and get them paid fairly. Under increasing pressure, and with *Superman* on its way to movie theaters, DC relented; they paid Siegel and Shuster a yearly income for the rest of their lives and began printing the credit "Superman created by Jerry Siegel and Joe Shuster" in every comic book.

Joe Shuster died at the age of 78 in 1992; Jerry Siegel died at the age of 81 in 1996. Although they spent decades fighting for fair compensation, they did live to see their hero—created when both men were just 23—dominate popular culture for almost 60 years.

CHAPTER 3

JACK KIRBY

IT'S EASY TO SEE WHY HE'S NICKNAMED THE "KING OF COMICS"; NO AMERICAN COMIC BOOK CREATOR COULD HOPE TO MATCH THE SUPERHUMAN SPEED, ENERGY, AND GRANDEUR OF THE WORK OF JACK KIRBY—MONSTER ARTIST EXTRAORDINAIRE, INVENTOR OF THE ROMANCE COMIC, CREATOR OF THE NEW GODS, AND COCREATOR OF CAPTAIN AMERICA, BLACK PANTHER, THE HULK, THOR, THE AVENGERS, THE X-MEN, AND THE FANTASTIC FOUR.

Jacob Kurtzberg was a Jewish boy growing up poor in Manhattan's Lower East Side in the 1920s. Kids from his block would roam the neighborhood, fighting gangs on other streets; sometimes Jacob would even take the subway to far-flung neighborhoods and learn how they rumbled in other parts of town. This violent childhood—combined with a storyteller's restless imagination, an insatiable need to draw, the struggles of finding work during the Depression, and fighting in World War II—shaped Jacob

Jack Kirby as a little boy

Kurtzberg, a quick-tempered fighter, to become Jack "King" Kirby, one of the most prolific comic book creators of all time!

Knowing their son's taste for violence, Rose and Benjamin Kurtzberg (immigrants from Austria) encouraged his interest in art—anything to keep him out of trouble. Jacob was still a teen when he first worked to bring in money for the family, drawing newspaper comic strips and public service cartoons, then joining Fleischer Studios to work in animation. The job was tedious and repetitive, and when the company moved to Florida, he stayed in New York. Soon Jacob found himself at Fox Feature Syndicate, answering an ad for an artist job.

Victor Fox was an accountant at National Allied Publications; the minute he saw the sales figures for *Action Comics* #1, he quit his

Joe Simon and Victor Fox

job and, with dollar signs in his eyes, opened a syndicate, hiring speedy artists like Jacob to churn out cheap Superman knockoffs to sell to publishers. Joe Simon, a sports cartoonist, joined Fox as an editor. Joe and Jacob hit it off, and they worked together constantly; Joe raced to come up with story ideas as quickly as the unstoppable Jacob would draw them. But Joe had a mind for business; he invited Jacob to join his freelance studio, drawing their own comics during lunch breaks and days off. To keep his side work a secret, Jacob Kurtzberg took on a pen name…and Jack Kirby was born.

Simon and Kirby connected with the publisher Martin Goodman and his new company, Timely Comics. Goodman, always eager to cut costs, sidestepped the syndicate go-betweens and hired Simon and Kirby directly. War was underway in Europe, which, in early 1941, the U.S. hadn't yet joined. That didn't stop Simon and Kirby from debuting their new character on the cover of *Captain America Comics* #1, punching Adolf Hitler in the face—a thrilling Kirby drawing, bursting with energy, as Captain America dives, pitched forward, deflecting Nazi bullets with his shield.

Simon had negotiated royalties on their deal so he and Kirby would earn a cut of the sales. The series was a huge hit, but Timely claimed that after the costs of printing, shipping, etc.,

Captain America hadn't made any money—a common scam to avoid paying creators their share. Simon and Kirby resorted again to their sideline, working freelance from a nearby office. They started selling stories to Timely's major competitor, National, but Goodman found out and fired them.

Kirby was drafted into the military in 1943 and sent to Europe, seeing some of the bloodiest, deadliest combat of the war. He was proud to fight against Hitler and always bragged that he'd killed four Nazis. But the horrors of combat gave him nightmares for the rest of his life.

Simon and Kirby reunited after the war. They realized that there was a genre of comic book no one had done yet, so they pioneered it; *Young Romance* started the romance comics craze in 1947, but their partnership wouldn't last much longer. The mid-'50s censorship crusade of the Comics Code drove publishers and studios out of business, and Simon and Kirby parted ways.

With no place else to work, Kirby returned in 1956 to the publisher that had fired him, Timely, which by then was called Atlas Comics, soon to become Marvel. There he drew short comics about giant monsters (with names like Goom, Xemnu the Titan, Fin Fang Foom, and most famously, in 1960, the tree-like Groot, "the Monster from Planet X") alongside writer/editor Stan Lee (more on Stan Lee on page 30). Kirby suspected that Lee told Martin Goodman about his side work for National and got him fired, and he swore he'd never work with Lee again. Ironically, all through the 1960s, Jack Kirby and Stan Lee would go on to share the most fruitful partnership in comic book history…even if Kirby wanted to kill Lee half the time.

The collaboration between Jack Kirby and Stan Lee was nothing short of legendary. Starting in 1961, Kirby and Lee created the Fantastic Four, Doctor Doom, the Silver Surfer, Galactus, Black Panther and his nation of Wakanda, the Inhumans, the X-Men, Magneto, and the Hulk. They updated the ancient Norse myths of Thor, Loki, and Asgard and banded their individual heroes together with a revitalized Captain America to form the Avengers.

Kirby and Stan Lee

But Kirby found it difficult working with Stan Lee, who claimed more than his share of credit for the bombastic ideas and characters that Kirby's nonstop pencil brought to life. Stifled and unable to flex his creative muscles, Kirby made a huge splash in 1970 by "crossing the street" back to National, now called DC Comics, where he was given a chance to create without limitations, not just drawing but writing his own comics.

This was Jack Kirby turned up to maximum volume. In his ambitious "Fourth World" storyline—a set of four interconnected series, *The New Gods*, *Mister Miracle*, *The Forever People*, and *Superman's Pal Jimmy Olsen*—Kirby explored a cosmic saga that he'd been toying with since his days at Marvel drawing *Thor* and

The Inhumans. It was the psychedelic space epic of two worlds at war, one good and one evil, fought by cosmic super-beings, when the long-running conflict finally reaches Earth.

Unfortunately, DC canceled the Fourth World comics before the story's climactic ending. Kirby returned to Marvel in 1975 and took another swing at the grand epic of his dreams, this time in the form of *The Eternals*: the story of god-like heroes and villains, the Eternals and the Deviants, and the mysterious alien giants called Celestials who created them five million years ago. *The Eternals* was also canceled before Kirby could finish the saga. By 1978, Kirby left Marvel once and for all.

For the next 15 years, after moving to California, Kirby designed characters like *Thundarr the Barbarian* for the Hanna-Barbera animation studio, designed toys, helped visualize sci-fi epics for Hollywood, and wrote and drew comics for smaller publishers. Like so many creators of American superhero comic books, he spent much of his later years fighting for his rights—the return of his original artwork from Marvel and DC and a fairer share of the profits from his creations.

Fittingly, Jack Kirby always envisioned that his comic books could become movies of remarkable scope and grandeur. Even when most cartoonists thought the work they drew was embarrassing, juvenile, and disposable, Kirby foresaw astonishing cinematic superhero epics like we have today. He died at the age of 76 in 1994, far too soon to see his creations on the screen.

CHAPTER 4

STAN LEE

EXCELSIOR!

MARVEL COMICS

"FACE FRONT, TRUE BELIEVERS!" THAT WAS JUST ONE OF THE WAYS STAN LEE ADDRESSED HIS LOYAL COMIC BOOK READERS. BY FORGING A PERSONAL CONNECTION WITH FANS, MARVEL'S LEGENDARY WRITER, EDITOR, PUBLISHER, AND SPOKESPERSON BECAME AS FAMOUS AS THE CHARACTERS HE COCREATED...AND MADE ENEMIES ALONG THE WAY.

Stan Lee is an oddity among superhero creators. People like Jerry Siegel, Joe Shuster, and Jack Kirby were underappreciated and underpaid, but their reputations grew as later generations came to value the enormity of their genius. Lee enjoyed decades of fame, wealth, and accolades…only to have his legacy reexamined and diminished in later years.

Stan Lee

Did Stan Lee deserve that, or was it a seesaw effect tied to Jack Kirby—when one was down, the other was up? As Stan might say…*keep readin'*!

Born Stanley Lieber in 1922, the son of Jewish Romanian immigrants, Lieber grew up in the Bronx during the Depression and took every job he could find, even writing newspaper obituaries. Finishing high school at age 16, he wanted to write; lucky for him, his cousin Jean Solomon married a publisher—Martin Goodman.

It was 1939; Superman made costumed heroes a craze. Goodman, age 28, started a comic book publisher to cash in. He hired Lieber as an apprentice who'd go for coffee, go for lunch…a "gofer." Lieber worked at Timely Comics—later renamed Atlas, and later Marvel—for 50 years.

One of Lieber's duties was writing backup stories so comic books qualified as "magazines" for lower shipping costs. He took the

Alex Schomburg and Jack Binder

name "Stan Lee," half-joking that he intended to be a great novelist and wouldn't taint his name with comic books. Soon he cocreated his first hit, the Destroyer, with artists Alex Schomburg and Jack Binder. He was beginning to excel, and Goodman made him editor in chief…at age 19.

In 1960, Lee was nearly 40 and ready to quit. He and Jack Kirby were collaborating on monster comics, teen melodrama, and sci-fi, but Goodman wanted a superhero team, like National's best-seller, *Justice League of America*. Lee told his wife, Joan, he was fed up, but she suggested he write the kind of comic he'd always wanted, something that hadn't been done.

Lee invented a team that was also a family, with bickering and money problems—superheroes appalled by the horrific transformation of their bodies. He assigned the script to Kirby, and the Fantastic Four were born!

Kirby and Lee

That's one account—the version Lee told. The other was Kirby's: Goodman decided to shutter Marvel; as furniture was carted away, Kirby told Lee to stall Goodman and plotted and drew a 25-page comic with all-new characters in a matter of days.

Whichever story is true, 1961's *Fantastic Four* #1 launched our era of true-to-life superheroes and revolutionized popular culture. It featured an arrogant, uptight leader, Mister Fantastic, that some compared to Lee, and the Thing, a cigar-chomping, two-fisted brawler, like Kirby. The first thing these two heroes did with their powers was to fight each other. Whoever had the idea, it certainly feels like Kirby's take.

Fantastic Four was the first time Lee worked in "the Marvel method"; he would write a one-page plot—sometimes shorter—then entrust it to an artist to flesh out the story. When the art was done, Lee wrote dialogue and narration. This made Marvel truly artist-driven, relying on contributors like Kirby, Steve Ditko, John Buscema, and more to tell stories and make crucial creative choices. It also makes it extremely difficult to pinpoint just what Stan Lee did—or didn't—create.

John Buscema

Fantastic Four was a superhero comic that combined virtually every other Lee/Kirby genre—teen melodrama, sci-fi, monsters—

just in the first issue. It began Marvel's period of unmatched creative innovation; within a few years, Lee and Kirby created the X-Men, Thor, the Hulk, Ant-Man, and the Wasp. In the pages of *Fantastic Four* they updated a classic character, Namor, and introduced Black Panther, Doctor Doom, the Silver Surfer, Galactus, the Watcher, and the Inhumans. From an idea by Lee and a Kirby design, Lee's brother, Larry Lieber, and artist Don Heck created Iron Man. Then Lee and Kirby banded their heroes together in the crossover sensation *The Avengers* #1. (This publication model inspired Marvel Studios to introduce heroes in separate movies starting in 2008, teaming them up in *The Avengers* in 2012.)

Steve Ditko

Another great Lee collaborator was Steve Ditko; they cocreated Spider-Man in 1962 and Doctor Strange in 1963. But the debate over credit hounded Lee. He insisted he came up with the ideas; artists just interpreted them. Ditko maintained that all Lee supplied was a name, "Spider-Man," and Ditko spun the entire web—spider bite, wall-crawling, web-shooters, everything. Lee admits the most memorable detail of Spider-Man's debut (*Amazing Fantasy* #15, August 1962) was an afterthought; when pages came back for script, there was extra room in the very final panel, so Lee tossed in an extra line of narration: "And a lean, silent figure slowly fades into the gathering darkness, aware at last that in this world, with great power there must also come—great responsibility!" The remark wasn't even attributed to Spidey's uncle Ben; that came later.

But Lee wrote more than scripts; he was the voice of "Bullpen Bulletins," chatting with fans, welcoming them into the office's chummy clubhouse atmosphere (a fiction Lee concocted, since most artists worked at home), replying to letters, and lecturing

on current events in his column, "Stan's Soapbox." This forum was crucial to Marvel's success; Lee created a sense of community that set the tone for fandom to this day. Another Lee feat: before *Fantastic Four* #1, comic books were strictly childish; Lee (who seemed a little embarrassed to work in juvenile entertainment) wrote teen and young adult heroes, grappling with big topics, for a teen and young adult readership. Suddenly Marvel was taken seriously by hip college students, artists, and filmmakers, a credit not only to innovative art by the likes of Kirby, Ditko, and Buscema, but to Lee's writing and tireless cheerleading.

Inevitably, as appreciation of Marvel's artists rose, it generated blowback for Lee, Marvel's smiling, energetic attention hog. He was quick to claim credit for ideas that were, at best, collaborative—at worst, entirely someone else's. But the Marvel phenomenon, built largely on the art of Ditko, Kirby, and

Buscema, wasn't created exclusively by Ditko, Kirby, and Buscema. Without Lee's contributions, like "with great power there must also come—great responsibility," and without his ringleader showmanship, Marvel wouldn't be Marvel.

Lee stopped writing most of Marvel's comics when he replaced Goodman as publisher in 1972. He moved to California in 1981 and retired in the '90s, though he retained the honorary title of Publisher Emeritus, reportedly drawing a million-dollar salary and a percentage of Hollywood profits. That arrangement ended when the new chairman terminated Lee's contract with a $10-million buyout—a handsome payday, but much less than Lee would have made once Marvel Studios became a Hollywood powerhouse. From the late '90s until his death in 2018, at the age of 95, Lee kept busy, corunning new entertainment companies and producing comics and shows; sadly, none amounted to much. His legacy lives on nevertheless; Stan Lee and his collaborators impacted our culture so deeply that his voice resonates to this day. *'Nuff said!*

CHAPTER 5

STEVE DITKO

THE ACCLAIMED ARTIST OF UNNERVING, CREEPY SCIENCE FICTION AND HORROR COMICS TOOK AN UNLIKELY CAREER STEP AND COCREATED MARVEL'S MOST BELOVED SUPERHERO, SPIDER-MAN—ARGU-ABLY ONE OF THE THREE MOST POPULAR SUPER-HEROES IN THE WORLD, ALONGSIDE SUPERMAN AND BATMAN. THEN, AT THE HEIGHT OF HIS MARVEL FAME, STEVE DITKO SIMPLY...WALKED AWAY.

Steve Ditko, the Pennsylvania-born son of eastern European immigrants, shared a love of adventure comic strips with his father. When costumed heroes came along, Ditko became a particular fan of Will Eisner's *The Spirit* and of Jerry Robinson's work on *Batman*. He learned Robinson taught art in New York City and moved there in 1950 to study under his idol. By 1953, Ditko was finding freelance artist work, even helping out at the studio of Joe Simon and Jack Kirby.

Just a few months before the Comics Code upended the industry, Ditko began drawing chilling shorts in 1954 for anthologies like *Black Magic, Strange Suspense Stories,* and *This Magazine Is Haunted* at the small, thrifty publisher Charlton Comics, where he excelled at virtually every genre of the macabre. He drew horror, crime, and sci-fi stories replete with anxious, sweating faces and bulging eyeballs. A bout of tuberculosis sidelined Ditko, and he moved back home to recover. He returned to New York and to comics in 1955, on the other side of a generational divide when the industry nearly collapsed, and went to work for Atlas Comics with Stan Lee.

Ditko went on drawing sci-fi and horror shorts, written by Lee, in anthologies like *Tales of Suspense* and *Strange Worlds* (including one about an elderly couple named Uncle Ben and Aunt May who try to keep a sickly mermaid on land as an adopted child). One of these titles, *Amazing Adventures,* became Ditko's primary showcase and was eventually retitled *Amazing Adult Fantasy,* then simply *Amazing Fantasy*. By this time, in 1962, Atlas was called Marvel

Comics, and the fifteenth and final issue of *Amazing Fantasy* (August 1962) featured a departure from the usual sci-fi and horror shorts: an 11-page lead story by Lee and Ditko introducing a new character. "Like costume heroes?" asked Lee in the story's opening narration, addressing the reader directly with a tantalizing peek behind the scenes. "Confidentially, we in the comic mag business refer to them as 'long underwear characters'! And, as you know, they're a dime a dozen! But, we think you may find our **Spiderman** just a bit…different!" (In this first story, Lee hadn't started using the hyphen in Spider-Man that later became standard.)

The story behind Spider-Man's conception is, like so many accounts of Marvel's early history…fraught. As Lee told it, he had a vague idea for Spider-Man that he gave to Jack Kirby to develop; but Kirby delivered a heroic fantasy of a young man who finds a magic ring, turning him into a brawny bodybuilder with a web-firing gun. Dissatisfied, Lee turned to Ditko, instructing him on the approach to take instead.

Ditko, however, recalled that after Kirby's attempt, Lee only gave him the name "Spider-Man," and it was Ditko who came up with a teen boy, modeled after himself, who is a member of the high school science club. Spider-Man wore a dizzying costume covered in webs and—because the teen Peter Parker would wish to hide his youth—a full mask covering his head and face. Before Spider-Man, teenagers were sidekicks, never the hero. One of his worst enemies, the Green Goblin, was his friend's dad; Spidey was a kid fighting evil grown-ups.

It took a visual genius like Ditko to craft a hero and villains out of contradictions. He could climb walls, but daintily, by his fingertips and toes. Doctor Octopus, one of his strongest foes, was a pudgy, middle-aged man held aloft by mighty metal arms. Sandman, a muscular powerhouse who could take a punch without flinching, was just as likely to melt away at the slightest touch. And the Vulture was as bald, gaunt, and ugly as his namesake bird—all the more intimidating for this unexpected aspect.

Disagreement between Ditko and Lee only worsened, though it led to one of Spidey's defining traits. Because Ditko wanted heavy drama about a kid on his slog to manhood, Peter was always anguished. Lee, scripting pages after they were drawn, couldn't give those tortured faces fun, zippy dialogue like he wanted, but the mask concealed Peter's expressions, so Lee's Spidey cracked jokes nonstop. The unwitting result was a character we all aspire to be, escaping his everyday troubles to feel free and have fun, all while being a hero.

Tensions deepened with Doctor Strange, a character that Lee announced in a 1963 magazine interview, crediting Ditko with his creation, but with a dig: "The first story is nothing great, but perhaps we can make something of him. 'Twas Steve's idea." Strange's debut saw the good sorcerer leave his body, assuming astral form to enter the dreams of a suffering man…only to discover that the man's mental torment was caused by his own moral corruption. Strange lectured the man on his psychological rot.

Ditko himself had embraced a moral philosophy called Objectivism, a behavioral guideline championed by the writer Ayn Rand that allowed no wiggle room between good and evil; the idea that circumstances create gray areas between right and wrong was entirely rejected. Ditko likely intended to depict Doctor Strange and Spider-Man as Objectivist heroes—in Strange's lecture to the man he saves and in Peter Parker's evolution from the selfish boy who let his uncle die into the selfless man who will never again falter in his moral duties. Between creative disagreements and his own uncompromising philosophy, it's impossible to tell just what drove Ditko, who rarely gave interviews or explained himself (though he did publish personal comics and essays outlining his beliefs in later years, available only by mail order). After turning in the pages for *Amazing Spider-Man* #38, Ditko resigned.

From the late 1960s through the 1970s, Ditko bounced between DC Comics and his old home of Charlton. At DC he created corny but enduring, oft-revived characters like the Creeper, Shade the

Changing Man, and Hawk and Dove. For Charlton, he created the Question, another take on his ideal Objectivist hero—a two-fisted crime-buster in a suit and hat, with a mask rendering his face blank and featureless.

But Ditko's potentially most personal creation came in 1967 for an independent comic book called *witzend*, where he introduced an even more sharply drawn Objectivist vigilante: Mister A. With a calling card neatly split into solid halves of black and white, Mister A expressed the moral mantra of "A is A," explaining that black is black, white is white, and there is nothing in between—never gray.

Although Ditko faded into obscurity—largely by choice, since he could have coasted on Spider-Man fame for decades—the artist kept a studio in Manhattan. He was almost reclusive in his refusal to talk to fans or grant interviews, but if you knew where to look, you could walk right up to his office door and knock (and probably get it shut in your face).

Ditko spent the '80s and '90s drawing mostly forgettable work-for-hire comics at small publishers and occasionally for DC, Archie Comics, and even Marvel, where he cocreated Squirrel Girl in 1992. He retired from superhero comics in the late '90s and dedicated the rest of his life to his personal Objectivist comics and essays. Steve Ditko, who never married or had children, died in 2018 at the age of 90.

CHAPTER 6

OSAMU TEZUKA

THE FATHER OF MANGA, THE GODFATHER OF ANIME, THE JAPANESE WALT DISNEY. OSAMU TEZUKA EARNED MANY NICKNAMES, HONORS, AND AWARDS. THE ARTIST, ANIMATOR, AND FILM PRODUCER CREATED MORE THAN 150,000 PAGES OF COMICS ACROSS STYLES AND GENRES IN HIS 40-YEAR CAREER AND HELPED SHAPE JAPANESE CULTURE.

If you met Osamu Tezuka as a young man, studying medicine at Osaka University in 1945, and asked what his future held, he might have told you he'd be a doctor. He probably wouldn't mention that as a child, he drew so much that his mother erased the contents of his notebooks so he could reuse them; he certainly wouldn't have known he'd create more than 150,000 pages of comics and become an animation pioneer to rival Walt Disney.

Tezuka—or Tezuka-sensei as he'd be called in Japan, to mark his accomplishment and distinction—was born in Osaka Prefecture in 1928. His taste in the arts was encouraged by his mother, who took him to see dance and theater, and by his father, who showed him Disney movies like *Bambi* and Fleischer Studios cartoons like *Popeye* (which sometimes included animation by Jack Kirby).

He was already a budding cartoonist when he began his medical studies, and within two years, Tezuka was publishing comic strips as well as acting and play-ing music onstage. In 1947, Tezuka completed *Shin Takarajima* (*New Treasure Island*, loosely based on the novel by Robert Louis Stevenson), his first book-length work of comics, which, in the Japanese

idiom, are known as manga. As a creator of manga, Tezuka was called a *mangaka*. His speed and output were unstoppable.

New Treasure Island started a sensation, kicking off the golden age of manga. Still in medical school, Tezuka published several more tomes between 1947 and 1951.

Finishing school in 1952, Tezuka intended to pursue medicine and began working at a hospital. But the success of his first two major works changed all that. Serialized between 1950 and 1951 in *Shönen Magazine* (an anthology still around today), Tezuka published *Janguru Taitei* (*Kimba the White Lion*), and from 1951 to 1952, *Atomu Taishi* (*Ambassador Atom*), introducing his most beloved character, called Atom in Japan, but known elsewhere in the world as Astro Boy.

In the story, Dr. Tenma builds Astro Boy to replace his late son, Tobio. But Astro doesn't grow like a human child, so Tenma, rather callously, sells him to a circus. He is found and adopted by Dr. Ochanomizu of the Ministry of Science, who kindly supplies Astro with a robot family. To show his gratitude, Astro lends his tremendous robot powers when any menace arises.

Astro Boy made Tezuka the most successful cartoonist in Japan. He opened a studio with assistants and staff, producing manga at a furious pace. Following Astro's success with boys, Tezuka launched a serial from 1953 to 1956 in *Shojo Club*, a counterpart magazine for girls. *Ribon no Kishi* (*Princess Knight*) tells the story of a girl who craves swordfights and adventure after a mischievous angel accidentally put both a pink girl's heart and a blue boy's heart in her soul. The king and the titular princess,

Sapphire, pretend she's a boy so she can inherit the throne and save their kingdom from the evil duke who would otherwise take it over. The angel, Tink, comes to retrieve the boy heart, but Sapphire refuses to give it up. By today's evolving standards, the strict boy/girl binary and gender caricature may seem problematic. But *Princess Knight* reads as a progressive tale symbolizing the fluidity of gender—the things a child loves don't have to be just "girl stuff" and "boy stuff," and the color of their heart isn't necessarily determined by the body they're born in.

The animation industry was dawning in Japan, and the Toei studio adapted *Boku no Son Goku* (*Son-Goku the Monkey*), Tezuka's manga take on the famous Chinese epic, *Journey to the West*. The process sparked Tezuka's interest, and in 1961, he founded his own animation studio, Mushi Productions (named after Tezuka's favorite insect, the Osamushi beetle, which happened to have his name). Tezuka produced animated shows of his own characters in the 1960s, including Kimba, Princess Knight, and of course, Astro Boy…the first Japanese cartoon to air in other countries.

This success even gave Tezuka the chance to meet his hero, Walt Disney, who was a fan of the Astro Boy program.

Tezuka and Walt Disney

Animation was a laborious, time-consuming process; to save time, Tezuka devised a more efficient method—limiting what elements in a shot would move, and only animating those. When a character spoke, their head would remain still, but the mouth would move

and the eyes changed expression. A figure looking at something in the sky would stand frozen, moving only their arm to point up. By animating those parts instead of redrawing the entire figure in each frame, production moved much faster…and it launched a new era of animation. People called it *anime.*

In the years while Tezuka was focusing on anime (first at Mushi, later at another studio, Tezuka Productions), popular tastes in Japan shifted away from manga for boys and girls, toward a darker, more violent idiom called *gekiga*, for older readers who were more jaded. These were stories of crime, corruption, and moral decay, created by a younger generation of cartoonists. Despite all his fame and success, Tezuka saw his manga fall out of favor, and almost out of defiance, he dove into gekiga, publishing several remarkable books from the late 1960s to the late 1970s, shocking for the callousness and cruelty of their characters. Among many, there was *Ningen Konchuki* (*The Book of Human Insects*, 1971), about a woman who goes through life getting close to others, learning to reproduce their talents, then killing them and claiming their accomplishments; *Ayako*, 1973, a decades-long saga about a family rife with murder and betrayal, all seen through the eyes of their youngest member, Ayako, as she's abused and imprisoned; and *Mu* (*MW*, 1978), a gripping drama about a Catholic priest trying to stop a psychopath's rash of kidnapping and murder,

all while the two men are locked in a tortured love affair. Unsurprisingly, this came to be known as Tezuka's dark period, and the author found he was suffering from depression and anxiety. For someone so fully immersed in his work, he was sinking into the negativity; it would take brightness and positivity for him to pull himself back out. Tezuka's work by the late '70s and early '80s started to become more redemptive and optimistic. Two series in particular, serialized from the early '70s and both ending in 1983, moved in this direction: *Burakku Jakku* (*Black Jack*), the story of a scar-faced, unlicensed surgeon doing good deeds and righting wrongs, and *Buddha*, a loosely fictionalized biography of the Indian prince Siddartha Gautama as he grows toward enlightenment and becomes the Buddha.

In the 1980s, Tezuka finally returned to his favorite work, which he'd begun in 1954 and only revisited sporadically over the next several decades—*Hi no Tori* (*Phoenix*). The master mangaka considered *Phoenix* his life's work, and he finally set about completing it; each volume was set in an entirely different era, moving both backward and forward in time. Like the fiery bird of myth, *Phoenix* was a story of reincarnation. Unfortunately, he published only 12 volumes; his death from stomach cancer left the cycle unfinished. Tezuka died in 1989 at the age of 60.

CHAPTER 7

HERGÉ

GEORGES REMI WAS A BOY SCOUT WITH AN INSATIABLE DRIVE TO LEARN AND EXPLORE. HE BECAME A CARTOONIST, TOOK THE PEN NAME HERGÉ, AND GAVE THESE QUALITIES OF HIS OWN TO AN INTREPID, GLOBE-TROTTING BOY REPORTER—TINTIN.

Georges Remi's childhood was underprivileged. Born in 1907, the family lived in a small apartment in Belgium's capital city of Brussels; Georges wanted for attention that his mother, who suffered from clinical depression, couldn't provide. He became quick-tempered and restless, drawing in his books and acting out in violent ways. As a schoolboy, he found the body of a man who had hanged himself in the forest; morbidly fascinated by the suicide, he went home and made crude nooses, which he sold to other kids.

It's fascinating, in hindsight, to contrast this dark, turbulent up-bringing with the characters and stories Remi would create—the vivid, colorful, joyous *Adventures of Tintin*, a globe-spanning series of comic "albums" (as slim volumes are called in Europe) following the crusading boy reporter, his dog Milou (or Snowy, in English translations), and friends like Captain Haddock and Professor Calculus. *Tintin* comics not only brought fame to Remi, they popularized an art style that came to be associated with Belgium and Franco-Belgian comics, called clear-line style.

Remi embarked on that path when his parents, concerned about his penchant for trouble, transferred him to a strict Catholic school. There, Remi discovered scouting and began to draw strips recording his explorations. He signed them with a pen name, Hergé, formed by taking his initials, surname first—"R.G."—and pronouncing them phonetically (in French). Scouting magazines like *Le Boy Scout Belge* (*Belgian Boy Scout*) started publishing original work by Hergé, like his 1926–1929 serial, *Les Aventures de Totor* (*The Adventures of Totor*).

Hergé's *Totor* comics came to the attention of Norbert Wallez, a conservative priest, fan of the Italian Fascist dictator Benito Mussolini, and publisher of the Catholic magazine *Le Vingtième Siècle* (*The Twentieth Century*). Wallez hired Hergé at the magazine, then assigned him a children's supplement to oversee called *Le Petit Vingtième* (*The Little Twentieth*), complete with Hergé's original comics. In 1929, the teen reporter Tintin and his brave, loyal dog Snowy made their first appearance in *Petit Vingtième*.

Hergé drew in clear strokes of consistent line weight—no line was thicker or narrower than others. Rather than cross-hatching—tight grids of lines for shading—Hergé kept his art

Clear line   **Traditional style**

completely clear, with flat, uniform color. The Dutch cartoonist Joost Swarte coined the term *ligne claire* ("clear line") to describe this style of art. Countless artists in Belgium and Europe started drawing in this fashion, including Swarte himself.

The first Tintin serial was collected in a hardcover album in 1930; *Tintin au pays des Soviets* (*Tintin in the Land of the Soviets*) saw Tintin visit Russia to investigate and expose the Bolshevik government, causing Soviet assassins to give chase. The serial was so popular that *Vingtième Siècle* hired an actor playing Tintin to arrive in Brussels by train, to roaring, cheering crowds, timed to coincide with the hero's return in that day's comic.

Tintin's next adventure would cause a little more trouble; Wallez requested the colonial setting of the Belgian Congo, in Africa, to encourage patriotic sentiment in readers. Rather than depict Tintin's usual worldly curiosity and his earnest interest in exploring other cultures, the resulting volume, 1931's *Tintin au Congo* (*Tintin in the Congo*) was a colonialist nightmare, showing the Congolese people in a racist, condescending light. Although the story was successful upon release, critical backlash against it was absolute; Hergé drew a milder second edition in 1946. Today, publishers don't even include this volume in *Tintin* reissues.

Hergé went on to publish 22 more volumes of Tintin adventures, with considerably greater success and critical reception than the *Congo* debacle. A later story, *Le Lotus Bleu* (*The Blue Lotus*) in 1936, sent Tintin to China. Hergé crafted the story alongside a Chinese artist he'd befriended in Brussels, Zhang Chongren. In his honor, Hergé created the character of Chang, who becomes Tintin's great friend.

Europe was on the march to war, and Imperial Japan had invaded Manchuria, northern China, in 1931. Japan would go on to join the Axis powers with Germany in 1941, amid the ongoing Japan-China War, causing China to side with the Allied forces. Hergé struck at this precise moment, just as that history was about to unfold, with a story denouncing Japan's presence in China and its imperialist expansion. (Sadly, as war loomed, Zhang had to return to China; he and Hergé wouldn't see each other again for 40 years.) In a similar fashion, Tintin's 1939 adventure, *Le Sceptre d'Ottokar* (*King Ottokar's Sceptre*), was a satirical story set in a fictional country that criticized the expansion of Nazi Germany as it absorbed Austria. In the months after the book's release, Germany would invade Poland and begin World War II in earnest.

Hergé's worst fears came to pass; Germany occupied Brussels in 1940, shutting down *Vingtième Siècle*. *Le Soir*, run by German agents, invited Hergé to publish *Tintin* there instead, asking also

that he become an informant for the Nazis. Hergé refused to collaborate but did publish in *Le Soir*. Though he was no Nazi sympathizer, this association brought him criticism and scorn. At war's end, the Allies shut down *Le Soir* and arrested many of its workers, even executing some. Hergé was arrested and barred from working for months; only the friendly intervention of Raymond LeBlanc, a respected businessman (and former member of the resistance), restored Hergé's good name.

LeBlanc installed Hergé in a new weekly *Tintin* magazine in 1946. It was a great success for the cartoonist, but the sudden volume of work (and influx of funding) drove him to open a studio with several assistants. His obsessive, driven way of working caused

Hergé great distress; he developed eczema, a painful skin condition, in his hands, which kept him from drawing, and he became depressed and had terrible nightmares. In 1948, perhaps during a nervous breakdown, Hergé simply disappeared. Nobody knew where he was, but Hergé had left Belgium for Lake Geneva, Switzerland; he stayed away for a whole year.

Returning to Brussels, Hergé enjoyed decades of success. From 1950 to 1953, he serialized two further Tintin volumes, *Objectif Lune* (*Destination Moon*) and *On a marché sur la Lune* (*Explorers on the Moon*), two of Tintin's funniest and most dazzling adventures. Putting approximately 11 assistants to work, these books featured astonishing visuals, such as the full-page reveal of the distinctive red-and-white rocket ship that Professor Calculus built to bring Tintin and Captain Haddock with him to the moon. A later volume, *Tintin au Tibet* (*Tintin in Tibet*, 1960) gave Hergé the opportunity to illustrate stark, white, snowy vistas and a monstrous Yeti, ridding himself of the lifeless white void of his dreams. It also led the artist to Asian sources that might help locate his friend Zhang.

After years of asking and searching, Hergé finally tracked him down, though it would take years before Zhang could leave China and meet his old friend again, in 1981. By this time, Hergé had been diagnosed with cancer of his bone marrow. He was too weak to draw regularly and never finished the volume he'd begun in 1978, *Tintin et l'alph-art* (*Tintin and Alph-Art*), set in Brussels' modern art scene. Hergé died in 1983, at the age of 76.

CHAPTER 8

FLO STEINBERG

MARVEL'S ORIGINAL "GAL FRIDAY" WAS MORE THAN A SECRETARY; "FABULOUS FLO" STEINBERG HELPED STAN LEE RUN THE PUBLISHER WHEN IT WAS JUST THE TWO OF THEM, BECAME A FOUNDING MEMBER OF THE FAMED MARVEL BULLPEN, AND OVERSAW A GROUNDBREAKING COMIC BOOK OF HER OWN.

"Oh, Stan, do you have a few minutes?"

"For our fabulous gal Friday? Sure. Say hello to the fans, Flo Steinberg!"

"Hello, fans, it's very nice to meet you. As Marvel's corresponding secretary, I feel as though I know most of you from your letters."

These words marked Florence Steinberg's entrance on *Voices of Marvel*, a record the comic book publisher mailed to members of its brand-new fan club, the Merry Marvel Marching Society, in 1965. The Massachusetts native moved to New York City in 1963, a few years after finishing college, and got help from an employment agency to look for a job; the agency sent her to a magazine publisher. Despite the parent company's innocuous name, Magazine Management, Steinberg landed at Marvel Comics.

At the time, Marvel was a one-person operation, where publisher and editor Stan Lee managed a corps of freelance artists (and did most of the writing personally). Referring to her as his "gal Friday" (after the man who aided in the title character Robinson Crusoe's survival, in the 1719 novel by Daniel Defoe), Lee depended on Steinberg to…well, basically run everything: manage the phones, send and read mail, track assignments, pressure artists to deliver their pages on time, and get freelancers paid. Steinberg also read fan letters, answered the phone when readers called with questions and unsolicited remarks about recent stories, and greeted all the visitors, wide-eyed kids, and aspiring freelancers who turned up at the door. "Fabulous Flo," as Lee called her (in the merry Marvel tradition of giving alliterative nicknames to staff) did all this with a sunny disposition and daffy demeanor that quickly endeared her to Marvel staff, fans, and fellow comic book creative types.

Marvel would eventually staff up and add more people in-house, but even when they did, the notion of the legendary "Marvel Bullpen"—a chummy atmosphere of comic book artists, writers, colorists, letterers, and production staff all working elbow-to-elbow at neighboring desks in the heart of Midtown Manhattan—was a fantasy that Stan Lee made up in his editorial pages, the "Bullpen Bulletins" at the back of every Marvel comic book. Nevertheless, the allure of the imaginary Marvel Bullpen was more real than reality; even though the bullpen clubhouse didn't quite exist—Jack Kirby was at home, probably shirtless, drawing *Fantastic Four* at his drafting table in Long Island, only putting on a shirt and tie to come into the office once in a while to turn in pages and pick up the next script—the Marvel Bullpen was a powerful and compelling symbol to represent Marvel's formidable artists and editors. In 1978, Kirby immortalized "the original Marvel Bullpen" in the comic book *What If?*, which imagined unlikely alternate stories for the company's best known characters.

What If? number 11—with its full title, *What If the Original Marvel Bullpen Had Become the Fantastic Four?*—sees a strange alien artifact come by mail to the Marvel offices. Hanging out together in Stan Lee's office when they open the package and unwittingly activate the device, these four bullpenners are doused in radiation and take on the powers of the Fantastic Four: the bombastic, boastful, take-charge Stan Lee turns into his own version of Mister Fantastic; production manager Sol Brodsky bursts into flame as the hot-headed Human Torch; Jack Kirby fully becomes the Marvel character that colleagues and fans always associated with him the most, the Thing; and Fabulous Flo herself is there to turn into Invisible Girl (the character, eventually renamed Invisible Woman, who many writers and commentators argue is the FF's most powerful member, after all).

But that would all come years later; in the intervening time, Steinberg had finally left Marvel in 1968, after a tenure of five years keeping the machine oiled and running. As Marvel became more and more successful during their decade of biggest and fastest growth, she was worn down by constant hard work; more and more fans were always calling and writing and dropping in. When the company didn't give her a raise of five dollars, Steinberg moved on.

The story of Fabulous Flo definitely doesn't end there, of course. Steinberg possessed a keen eye for talent, intelligence, and potential, and she had helped recruit her assistant at Marvel, Linda Fite, who would go on to become a writer of comics herself and a full-time Marvel employee in many capacities. Steinberg also befriended Trina Robbins, a cartoonist and writer (who would go on to become the first female artist to draw Wonder Woman); through Robbins, Steinberg learned about the burgeoning world of underground comics, a scene referred to as "comix"—wild, rude, unruly, black-and-white comics that railed against authority and mocked a society that oppressed women, minorities, and the poor.

Linda Fite

A restless and vivacious lover of life, a seeker of adventure, Steinberg moved around for a few years; after a buttoned-down job in communications for the oil industry, she moved to the beating heart of underground comix, San Francisco, California. After that, she spent a little time back home in the Boston area, then returned with friends to New York and went back to working in comics, at a division of Warren Publishing, a maker of horror-comic magazines. It was there and then that Steinberg's years of connections and relationships within comics led her to her next venture.

Pairing her phone book full of prominent comic book artists with her new passion for underground comix, Steinberg brought together an all-star roster of cartoonists and oversaw the one-shot *Big Apple Comix* in 1975. A black-and-white anthology of short stories set in New York City—the "Big Apple" of the title— Steinberg's comic book was raunchy, irreverent, highly satirical, and definitely just for adults, as the cover warned. *Big Apple Comix* was one of the biggest, most visible publications to come out of underground comix yet and an important early work in the birth of "independent" comics—comic books that found distribution channels and a readership outside the confines of the big comic book publishers.

Fabulous Flo Steinberg is rightly remembered and loved for so many reasons, including her role building modern Marvel, her lifelong dedication to comics, and her pioneering work in the medium's alternative scenes. She was also a warm, personal friend to several generations of Marvel editors and staff, and a particular inspiration to the women who followed in her footsteps and joined the publisher in the following decades. Steinberg returned to Marvel in the 1990s and worked there as a proofreader for the rest of her life. She died in 2017 at the age of 78.

CHAPTER 9

WILL EISNER

ONE OF THE GREATEST ARTISTS OF COMICS' GOLDEN AGE IS ALSO CONSIDERED THE FATHER OF THE GRAPHIC NOVEL. FOR BETTER OR WORSE, WILL EISNER POPULARIZED THE TERM THAT WOULD CONFER PRESTIGE ON COMIC BOOKS FOR DECADES TO COME.

Born in Brooklyn in 1917 to Jewish European immigrant parents, Eisner's father, Shmuel, fled Austria-Hungary, and his mother, Fannie Ingber, came from Romania. She hoped Will and his siblings would have a good education and enjoy better lives, and she was dismayed when Will gravitated toward art and film, which seemed like hopeless prospects to her.

After drawing for the student paper and designing theater sets at the Bronx's DeWitt Clinton High School (where he was friends with future Batman creator Bob Kane; Stan Lee would attend later, as well), Eisner trained at the Art Students League of New York and started landing his first illustration jobs, drawing for newspapers and pulp magazines. In 1936 Bob Kane, who was drawing comic strips, introduced Eisner to Jerry Iger, the editor of *Wow, What a Magazine!* Iger hired Eisner to write and draw comic strips; when the magazine folded after four issues, Eisner and Iger went into business together.

Formally calling their studio Eisner & Iger—also known by the names Universal Phoenix Feature Syndicate and Syndicated Features Corporation—the partners found immediate success packaging their own comics to sell to

Eisner and Jerry Iger

publishers. Eisner was fast, and his skills were diverse—so much so, that he cranked out pages in totally different art styles, under pen names, claiming they were the work of five different artists in order to make their studio seem bigger and more formidable. By the end of the '30s, Eisner and Iger were selling huge amounts of work and making money despite the crushing hardship of the Depression. They could afford to hire freelancers, at different times providing work and artistic mentorship to a young, pre-"Jack Kirby" Jacob Kurtzberg and to Steve Ditko.

One of Eisner's principal clients was Victor Fox and his Fox Feature Syndicate. Fox hired him in 1939 to write and draw a *Superman* rip-off called *Wonderman*; when this landed Fox in court, sued by National Allied Publications, he ordered Eisner to lie and claim it was his original creation. They still lost the suit, and Eisner quit. (Fox tried to lure away some of Eisner's stable of artists, unaware that most of the cartoonists he was reaching out to were pseudonyms of Eisner himself; one freelancer who did see Fox's ad and turned up looking for work was Jacob "Jack Kirby" Kurtzberg.)

The same year, Quality Comics came scouting for talent. Newspaper publishers wanted to capitalize on the comic book boom, and Quality's chief, Everett Arnold, needed writer-artists to create full-color supplements to insert in Sunday papers. What happened next was…well, it was the opposite of what Jerry Siegel and Joe Shuster went through when they sold *Superman* to National. Eisner presented a contract to Arnold guaranteeing he retained full ownership of his creations. Arnold agreed, and Eisner ended his partnership with Jerry Iger to open his own studio dedicated exclusively to Quality Comics and selling Iger his half of the Eisner & Iger enterprise at a profit.

Eisner created a handsome crime fighter in a rumpled blue suit and hat—the Spirit. Arnold's would-be newspaper clients liked it but asked if the Spirit would don a costume. Tired of superheroes, Eisner said, "Yes, he has a costume!" and added a slim black mask around his eyes (a detail of the Spirit's conception that Eisner revealed in a magazine interview decades later).

The Spirit was a smash. It followed the adventures of a police detective, Denny Colt, believed killed in action. The hero, very much alive, hid his identity behind a domino mask and continued to fight crime, known only as the Spirit. Even more memorable, the comic was formally inventive; Eisner experimented freely with panel structure, logo design, and lettering. Titles could appear in giant letters that formed part of the scene being depicted; characters might walk (or fall) from one panel into another.

Eisner continued to employ and mentor promising young talent. Among others, he had artistic help on *The Spirit* from Jack Cole, the dazzlingly talented cartoonist who later created Plastic Man, and from Wally Wood, a soon-to-be legendary EC

Jack Cole and Wally Wood

Comics illustrator in *Mad* and other titles, one of the visionaries of Topps's grisly Mars Attacks! trading cards, and a formative artist on Marvel's *Daredevil*.

Later in his career, Eisner moved even further from heroes, telling true-to-life stories of Jewish life in New York City in book-length comics like 1978's *A Contract with God and Other Tenement Stories*. The collection of tales set in one apartment building on the Lower East Side, particularly the main story about a religious man whose faith is shaken by the death of his daughter, was inspired by the death of Eisner's own young daughter from leukemia in 1970. Follow-up books explored the tenement setting, and later books by Eisner shifted to literary and historical subject matter.

The cover of *Contract with God* presented the book as "a graphic novel by Will Eisner"—the first time the term "graphic novel" was used in such a prominent fashion, though the historian Richard Kyle had coined it nearly 15 years earlier. *Contract with God* was published exclusively in its bound book form, never serialized, and Eisner's wish to convey that this was designed as a single work— centrally linked by theme and narrative—led to widespread use, even overuse, of the term "graphic novel" for other books in that idiom.

So monumental was the quality and influence of Eisner's work that the American comic book industry named its most prestigious honors after him; the Will Eisner Comics Hall of Fame and the Will Eisner Comic Industry Awards were founded in 1988. The coveted Eisner Award is conferred on outstanding work in every field of comic book making at a ceremony held yearly at San Diego Comic-Con.

There's no shortage of lasting impact from the career of Will Eisner, but the last and among his most important legacies was his role as an educator. To arrive at a precise meaning of the imprecise term "comics," Eisner coined the phrase "sequential art"—drawings shown in series, to simulate events unfolding in time—and gave lectures on the craft at universities and art schools. Eisner also taught at New York's School of Visual Arts, which carries on his tradition of training in comics today, and published two essential textbooks on the discipline of creating comics: *Comics and Sequential Art* in 1985 and *Graphic Storytelling and Visual Narrative* in 1996. Eisner died in 2005 at age 87.

His mother would have been proud.

**Will Eisner
Comics Hall
of Fame Award**

**Will Eisner Comic
Industry Award**

CHAPTER 10

MARIE SEVERIN

THOUGH NEVER AS WELL KNOWN AS HER MALE PEERS, THE VERSATILE MARIE SEVERIN WAS ONE OF MARVEL'S MOST RESOURCEFUL DESIGNERS, ARTISTS, AND HUMORISTS, AS WELL AS A COLORIST WHO SET THE TONE FOR EC'S BLOOD-SPATTERED HORROR AND CRIME COMICS.

Marie Severin was drafted into the business on short notice when her older brother, the EC Comics artist John Severin, a distinguished illustrator of war and western titles and a contributor to the humor comic *Mad*, needed a colorist. Born in Long Island and raised in Brooklyn, the Severins had come from an artistic upbringing—their father was a Norwegian immigrant and World War I veteran who worked as a packaging designer for a cosmetics company, and both parents encouraged their children's artistic talents, so the younger Severin was already a skilled artist when the call came.

Severin's first published coloring work was the title *A Moon, a Girl…Romance* #9 in 1949, when she was 20. From there, Severin went on to color virtually everything at EC, including the full line of war comics overseen by cartoonist and editor Harvey Kurtzman, and most famously, the company's graphic crime and horror comics. Applying her own critical eye, Severin would choose whether to deepen the crimson hues of blood and gore or render them brighter for clarity or more muted whenever a scenario looked gruesome enough to frighten off disapproving parents.

In the fast-paced, catch-as-catch-can environment of publishing and comic books, EC frequently had need of quick, last-minute fixes, and Severin was called upon to draw and make corrections for touch-ups on other artists' pages. These skills, as much as Severin's vast repertoire of talents, ensured the position she would go on to hold in comics for decades.

The near collapse of the comic book industry following the 1954 Senate Subcommittee Hearings on Juvenile Delinquency hit EC Comics hard and made it difficult for Severin to find work. She did a little freelance for Atlas Comics, the predecessor to Marvel, and ended up working full-time as a Marvel production artist in 1959, where she'd continue to work until the 1990s. A splashy illustration by Severin for the magazine *Esquire* so impressed Marvel's editor in chief Stan Lee that he assigned Severin to take over drawing the Doctor Strange feature in the anthology series *Strange Tales* in 1967. She had big shoes to fill—Severin's predecessors in the job had been Bill Everett, the creator of Namor the Sub-Mariner and cocreator of Daredevil, and before him, Strange's cocreator Steve Ditko himself. In the pages of *Strange Tales*, Severin and Lee cocreated an imposing cosmic figure, the Living Tribunal—an impartial, god-like judge balancing the scales of Marvel's multiple universes. It fell to the sorcerer Doctor Strange to convince the Living Tribunal that Earth had the potential to do good in the cosmos and should be allowed to go on existing.

In addition to drawing, Severin colored comics over other artists, even taking on the role of Marvel's head colorist beginning in the late 1960s. She had learned the craft studiously as a colorist at EC and only deepened her skill at Marvel; she grew so talented at the artful use of hue and contrast that many fellow artists considered her the finest colorist of the era.

One of Severin's duties as a production designer—still her full-time job title even as she drew *Strange Tales* and colored interiors for other titles—was to design cover layouts for other artists. Severin would rough out the composition for a piece before handing it to the artist of the comic to finish in pencil. The accolades for some of Marvel's memorable '60s and '70s covers were given to the artists who drew them, with no mention of Severin's influential role.

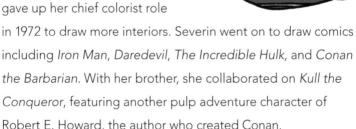

She also drew many comic book covers of her own and gave up her chief colorist role in 1972 to draw more interiors. Severin went on to draw comics including *Iron Man*, *Daredevil*, *The Incredible Hulk*, and *Conan the Barbarian*. With her brother, she collaborated on *Kull the Conqueror*, featuring another pulp adventure character of Robert E. Howard, the author who created Conan.

In 1976, Marvel introduced a new female character, Spider-Woman—seemingly a counterpart to Spider-Man, but with an unrelated backstory and unrelated abilities. In reality, Marvel rushed the character into development after it occurred to Stan Lee that another publisher might create such a character and claim rights to the name. DC and Marvel had been through that fight over their respective characters Wonder Woman and Wonder Man (not to be confused with the hackneyed Superman knockoff Wonderman whom Will Eisner created at Victor Fox's behest). The editor and writer Archie Goodwin came up with Spider-Woman's—a.k.a. Jessica Drew—origin and abilities, and Severin designed the character, dressing her in an eye-popping red suit with a yellow hourglass pattern down the front, like the markings of some deadly spider, and web-wings spanning from her wrists to her hips. A partial mask left her mouth and chin uncovered, with her eyes hidden behind white lenses. Despite initial success, and even an animated show, the character wasn't a favorite of fans, who considered her a Spider-Man knockoff. Nevertheless, she's still around in Marvel stories today; her look has undergone many transformations but she's always retained Severin's distinctive red-and-yellow patterning in some form and her stark white eyes.

For all of her accomplishments drawing, inking, and coloring serious, action-packed superhero adventures, Severin's most beloved work may be *Not Brand Echh*. From 1967 to 1969, Marvel published the satirical anthology, poking fun at Marvel's own comic books and those of other publishers, most prominent among them DC. Severin's artistic sense of humor stood out—her incisive caricatures of friends and coworkers were beloved around the Marvel offices, after all—and she held her own in the

Bill Everett, John Severin, and Gene Colan

comic alongside artistic talents like Bill Everett, her own brother John, and Gene Colan, the famed artist of *Daredevil*, *Tomb of Dracula*, and *Howard the Duck* and cocreator of the Falcon and Blade, the vampire hunter. *Not Brand Echh* is best remembered for Severin's covers and interior artwork.

Comic books have suffered from a shortage of female talent since their beginning, an imbalance that is only beginning to be righted in the 21st century. But the exceptional Marie Severin was invaluable to Marvel, not only at a time when women were almost totally absent from the industry, but in practically every artistic discipline she could exercise. As if to prove the assertion that a woman has to work harder than a man only to reach the same level of acceptance, Severin was overshadowed by her male contemporaries—pencilers, inkers, colorists, and production artists—even though she excelled at each of their jobs and more. She outlived her big brother, John, who died in 2012; Marie Severin died in 2018, after suffering a stroke, at the age of 89.

CHAPTER 11

RAMONA FRADON

MOST AMERICAN WOMEN DURING RAMONA FRADON'S TIME WERE HOUSEWIVES; FEW HAD CAREERS, LET ALONE CAREERS DRAWING COMIC BOOKS. FRADON STANDS OUT AS ONE OF COMICS' UNLIKELIEST STARS: THE BELOVED BUT RELATIVELY LITTLE-KNOWN ARTIST OF A BELOVED BUT FREQUENTLY MOCKED CHARACTER.

Like her contemporary Marie Severin, Ramona Fradon was a comic book artist overlooked and underappreciated by the public for decades—an artist's artist, well known and well loved by her peers and the publishers who employed her, but escaping the notice of most fans, who preferred artists like Superman's Curt Swan. It seems only

fitting, then, that Fradon should be most closely associated with a superhero that few people noticed or took seriously or even liked all that much—Aquaman. However, like Aquaman, Fradon eventually came into a long-overdue renaissance of popularity and appreciation.

Fradon was born in Chicago in 1926 and raised outside of New York City, where she studied at the prestigious Parsons School of Design. Shortly after graduating, she started to work in cartooning and comics; her talent was so huge and so evident that a friend showed her portfolio to editors at DC Comics, where she quickly got hired as an artist. Before long, she had landed a regular slot drawing Aquaman stories in the anthology series *Adventure Comics*.

Aquaman, who can breathe underwater and communicate with the creatures of the ocean, made his debut fairly early in modern comic book history. He already wore his signature green tights and a shirt of orange scales when he first appeared in the pages of *More Fun Comics* #73 in 1941, created by the editor and writer Mort Weisinger and the artist Paul Norris. But two decades later, it was Ramona Fradon's take on Aquaman as a smiling superhero with Hollywood good looks that defined the style of the character for decades to come—more boyish than Superman, with the reddish cheeks and sun-kissed blonde hair of a surfer who spends all his time on the beach and in the ocean. Her Aquaman inspired the design of the character as immortalized in *Super Friends*, the influential cartoon series that introduced generations of children to DC's heroes and villains. *Super Friends*, in turn, launched a popular line of toys, and Fradon's take on Aquaman ended up in the hands of children around the world.

During her time with the character, Fradon gave life to his undersea world and the aquatic creatures Aquaman swam among, befriended, and occasionally fought against—an ocean full of colorful octopuses, menacing sharks, friendly whales, schools of fish, resplendent coral reefs, and bubbles, lots of air bubbles blowing from the mouths of underwater animals. She also cocreated some of Aquaman's key supporting characters during this time, including his sidekick, Aqualad, and his mother, the queen Atlanna.

In 1959, Fradona became pregnant; she moved with her family to Connecticut to raise her daughter. In 1963, she went back to drawing for DC here and there, creating the oddball, shape-shifting superhero Metamorpho and the Element Man alongside writer

Bob Haney, and contributing to his stories off and on for the next decade. In 1972, she returned full-time to DC, drawing *Plastic Man* and other titles.

Unfortunately for Fradon, and for comic book fans everywhere, it was an era less welcoming to working mothers, and being a freelance comic book artist meant regularly traveling to the city to meet with editors and line up new assignments—tasks that are dispatched easily today over email—which Fradon couldn't juggle easily with her home life in Connecticut. As a result, Fradon took jobs less frequently than male artists, who could leave child care to their wives and dedicate a full-time workday schedule to meet the demands of the freelance life.

Ramona Fradon retired from comics in 1995 but continued to attend comic book conventions into her 90s, meeting fans, signing comics, drawing sketches, and selling commissioned art pieces. After decades as an underappreciated artist linked with an underappreciated superhero, few people were as surprised as Ramona Fradon, or as delighted, to witness Aquaman's resurgence as a major Hollywood movie star…and her own renaissance as one of the convention circuit's most beloved and sought-after artists.

CHAPTER 12

CHRISTOPHER PRIEST

THE FIRST AFRICAN AMERICAN WRITER AND EDITOR TO WORK IN MAINSTREAM AMERICAN SUPERHERO COMICS, CHRISTOPHER PRIEST WROTE ONE OF THE CRUCIAL, CHARACTER-DEFINING RUNS OF *BLACK PANTHER*. HIS SPOT IN COMIC BOOK HISTORY SHOULD BE ASSURED—BUT FOR DECADES, HE'S BEEN ALL BUT FORGOTTEN.

Comics have an extremely poor history when it comes to African American inclusivity. George Herriman, the creator of *Krazy Kat* (one of the most highly regarded strips in news-

George Herriman and Jackie Ormes

paper comics history, running from 1913 to 1944), was the New Orleans–born son of mixed-race Creole parents. Jackie Ormes, doubly exceptional in early comics history as a woman and an African American, did several successful comic strips beginning in 1937, most famously featuring the character Torchy Brown, a black fashion model. But these were extremely rare exceptions. For decades, the comics industry was almost totally bereft of creators of color. In superhero comics, occasional black freelance contributors turned up, but until Priest, none had worked at a major publisher as a writer or editor.

James Christopher Owsley—the man better known as Christopher Priest, by the fervent few who know him at all—was born in 1961 in Queens, New York. Jim Owsley joined Marvel Comics as an intern in 1978, still in high school. By 1979 he'd been brought on staff as an assistant editor, tasked with writing comics as well. An early writing job for Owsley was the four-issue miniseries *The Falcon*, starring Captain America's friend and brother-in-arms, Sam Wilson (the first African American superhero in comics, created 15 years earlier by Stan Lee and

Gene Colan). Owsley handled the character deftly, combining action and suspense with humor, which led Marvel to assign him *Power Man and Iron Fist*, costarring a black lead, Luke Cage, created in response to the "Blaxploitation" movies of the 1970s. Owsley noticed the pattern; he was being assigned black characters.

By Owsley's own admission, he was a better writer than an editor. His less-than-stellar job performance created friction because of  missed deadlines and poor communication, and he had arguments with coworkers and creative teams. Jim Shooter, the editor in chief, finally fired him. Owsley had been unhappy, and his termination came as a relief.

He briefly continued to write freelance for Marvel and wrote a few things for DC Comics, including Green Lantern in the pages of *Action Comics Weekly*, but both relationships ended bitterly, over tensions that Owsley chalked up to racism. He just wasn't liked at either publisher. Owsley quit comics and moved to New Jersey to work driving buses.

Mike Gold, an editor at DC Comics, perceived talent in Owsley nevertheless. Gold felt there was a racism problem in the comic book industry (and virtually every industry), which barred

African American talent from breaking in, prevented existing talent from rising, and drove promising talent away. It took a lot of cajoling, but Gold persuaded Owsley to take an editor job at DC in 1990, writing two Green Lantern miniseries as well. By then, Owsley had changed his name to Christopher Priest. Unfortunately, tensions arose once more, and Priest didn't stay at DC long. He quit comics again and focused on playing music, web design, novel writing, and ministry (ordained as a Baptist). His best work in comics, however, was still to come.

Former Marvel editor in chief (and Priest's original boss) Jim Shooter had cofounded a new publisher in 1989, Valiant Comics; Acclaim Entertainment bought the company in 1994. It was there that Priest teamed up in 1997 with M.D. Bright—his old Marvel collaborator on The Falcon and Power Man and Iron Fist, and at DC on Green Lantern: Emerald Dawn—to create what they billed as "the world's worst superhero team"…Quantum and Woody. The editor Fabian Nicieza wanted a "Power Man and Iron Fist"-style duo and had the idea to reunite the creative team. Bright was a bit wary but agreed as long as they made the white character, not the black character, the comic relief.

Eric Henderson and Woody Van Chelton were estranged child-hood friends who bickered over race (Eric was black; Woody, white), personality (Eric was serious and responsible; Woody, a joker and a bum), and romance (Woody had a fling with Eric's childhood crush, Amy Fishbein). They reunited, only to become trapped in an experimental quantum chamber, transforming their bodies into pure energy. Now two guys who could barely stand each other wore power bands that they had to "klang" together every 24 hours to keep their atoms from disintegrating. Eric adopted the superhero name Quantum; Woody, declaring that "Code names are stupid," elected to go by Woody.

Quantum and Woody was an extremely incisive comic, outstanding as an action/adventure series while also hilariously satirizing clichés of superhero comics and Hollywood action movies. Priest wrote stories in the form of looping, convoluted puzzles, slowly unpacking and teasing out details to reveal the full scenario. The comic became a cult sensation, fondly remembered by a generation of fans. The publisher Valiant Comics enjoyed a second life beginning in 2012, when new owners began a line-wide reboot; in addition to an updated version of Quantum and Woody by James Asmus and Tom Fowler, Priest and Bright returned in 2014 for a sequel, Q2: The Return of Quantum and Woody, picking up their characters decades later to explore how their lives had changed.

As the initial Quantum and Woody unfolded, Priest returned to write for Marvel in 1998. Jimmy Palmiotti and Joe Quesada launched an editorial imprint called Marvel Knights, consisting of four titles: Daredevil, Punisher, The Inhumans, and Black Panther. They called Priest; he was inclined to say no, for the same reason he'd grown tired of writing almost exclusively black characters the first time around—he worried black characters were all he'd ever be allowed—but he would accept if they'd let him hang the story on an unlikely white protagonist.

Stan Lee and Jack Kirby had depicted T'Challa as the monarch of his futuristic African kingdom; Priest inverted the formula, bringing Black Panther to New York City as a royal VIP who had to be handled—with great difficulty and no small amount of comedy—by Everett Ross, a government agent. (This original character would be the CIA man played onscreen by Martin Freeman in the movies *Captain America: Civil War* and *Black Panther*.) By taking T'Challa out of Wakanda, Priest cleverly found a way to make Black Panther even more impressive, as a suave, worldly mover and shaker. The influence of this run on Black Panther's onscreen adaptation is plain, and it remains one of the defining takes on the character, alongside Lee/Kirby's and the series relaunch by Ta-Nehisi Coates and Brian Stelfreeze.

And yet, when Priest's remarkable run of 62 issues ended, he spun off a follow-up series titled *The Crew* that was quickly canceled. Priest started to feel again that he'd only get a crack at characters of color and lower-tier superheroes, never a Superman. He got calls offering writing jobs on one black character after another, which he declined. His work in comics began to fade from sight again.

Recently, however, Priest finally seemed to have gotten the shot he always wanted. DC hired him to write a white protagonist in the 2016 series *Deathstroke: Rebirth*. On the strength of that, they gave him the reins to *Justice League*—his chance to write Superman.

One only hopes that this time, Priest is here to stay.

CHAPTER 13

TOVE JANSSON

A MULTIDISCIPLINARY GENIUS,
TOVE JANSSON—ILLUSTRATOR, COMIC STRIP
CARTOONIST, PAINTER, AND AUTHOR—
CREATED THE ENCHANTING WORLD OF THE
MOOMINS TO AMUSE CHILDREN. IN THE PROCESS,
SHE BECAME ONE OF FINLAND'S MOST
ACCLAIMED CITIZENS.

The eldest child of an entire family of artists, Tove Jansson was born in 1914 in Helsinki, which at that time was in the Grand Duchy of Finland (not the modern  country simply called Finland) and part of the bygone Russian Empire. Her father was a sculptor and her mother, an illustrator; her two younger brothers would grow up to become a photographer, and a cartoonist and author. Jansson, already surrounded by art at home, trained in it further in Sweden, Finland, and Paris.

Although Jansson would work in many artistic disciplines, including as an author, painter, illustrator, and cartoonist, her greatest fame in Finland and around the world derives from her creations, the Moomins, a family of plump characters with vaguely hippopotamus-ish snouts, and their friends and neighbors in Moominvalley. Despite their fantastical appearances, the Moomin characters were possessed of complex psychologies and rich inner lives, and they could be inferred to be based on Jansson herself and various people around her, including her parents, her friends, and her partner.

The Moomins were the stars of work published in multiple formats, including nine books of prose that were adorned throughout with illustrations, five picture books, and a series of comic strips that ran for 21 years, all of it created or overseen by

Tove Jansson. The characters have also been interpreted in film and TV animation, puppetry, theatrical productions, opera, and musical recordings. At the Moomin Museum in Finland, visitors can see 2,000 exhibits, including Jansson's paintings and illustrations, statues, miniatures, and a small-scale model of the Moomin House. Finland is also home to the Moominworld theme park, featuring a full-size, five-story Moomin House. There are additional Moomin theme parks in Japan—where Jansson and the Moomins enjoy fame and renown second only to Finland—and Moomin shops and cafés around the world. Moomins grace postage stamps in both Finland and Japan and are emblazoned on the sides of jet airliners for the Finnish airline Finnair. So beloved are the Moomins that they have become Finland's proudest cultural export.

It all began with a book that Jansson wrote to work out her anxiety in the wake of World War II. *Småtrollen och den stora översvämningen* (*The Moomins and the Great Flood*, published in 1945) began to introduce, through prose, these characters that would go on to take over the world. In the story, the protagonist Moomintroll (or simply Moomin, the child of the family, possibly based on Jansson herself) and Moominmamma wander through the woods to find their lost Moominpappa. They undergo a harrowing journey but face it with innocence and openness. Eventually they are reunited, far from their old home, arriving in a valley where Moominpappa has built a house for them to live. The second book, *Kometjakten* (*Comet in Moominland*, 1946), introduced many more of the characters living in Moominvalley and kicked off the series in earnest.

Jansson explained that she found herself feeling depressed at the end of World War II and wished to look at the world through a context of more naïveté and innocence. This was the perspective that informed the creation of the Moomins and that could be said to pose their defining characteristics.

Several more prose books followed, but it was in 1952 that Jansson expanded into her first picture book, fully illustrating the Moomins' adventures for the first time, with the unwieldy title of *Hur gick det sen? Boken om Mumlan, Mumintrollet och Lilla My* (*The Book About Moomin, Mymble and Little My*). In this installment, Moomintroll meets a new human character called the Mymble, whose sister, Little My, has gone missing. Moomintroll helps her look, and the sisters become a permanent part of the Moomin ensemble afterward.

Shortly after, in 1954, Jansson debuted *Moomin*, the comic strip, for English-language readers in the London newspaper the *Evening News*. Jansson wrote and drew it all herself for the first five years, then began sharing the work in 1959, assigning the writing to her youngest brother, the cartoonist Lars Jansson. In 1960,

Lars Jansson

Lars took over writing and drawing the *Moomin* comic strip entirely. At its peak, *Moomin* had over 20 million readers in more than 40 countries—Finland's most popular comic strip ever. Today, collected editions of the full run are available from the Canadian publisher Drawn & Quarterly.

While carrying on further art studies from the 1940s, Jansson met the Finnish American-born graphic designer Tuulikki Pietilä; they collaborated on many projects—with Pietilä even helping Jansson conceptualize the full-scale Moomin House—and they became romantic partners who stayed together until the end of Jansson's life. They traveled extensively together, all around the world, and spent summers on the island of Klovharu in the Finnish community of Pellinki. Jansson based a Moomin character on Pietilä, the dizzyingly high-energy Too-Ticky.

Tuulikki Pietilä

Between her Moomin prose and picture books, the comic strip, and her novels and books of short stories, Jansson became the most widely read Finnish author in the world. In 1966, she won the illustrious Hans Christian Andersen Award for writing, an honor that has been nicknamed the Nobel Prize of children's literature.

As the decade of the 1970s dawned, Jansson withdrew from working on the Moomins but continued painting and writing for the rest of her life. When not writing books, picture books, and comics for children, Jansson wrote six novels and five collections of short stories.

An animated Moomin series debuted in Japan in 1969, produced by the studio Zuiyo Enterprises for Fuji TV. This accounts for the Moomins' enormous popularity in Japan. In 1990, another anime series, *Moomin*, would debut. It was a Japanese/Dutch coproduction, overseen by Lars Jansson and his daughter Sophia. *Moomin* ran for 104 episodes and was the first TV series of the Moomin characters to be distributed internationally.

Tove Jansson died in 2001, at the age of 86, but her Moomins are arguably more beloved today than ever, with a second theme park in Japan and a new animated TV series, *Moominvalley*, adding to Jansson's considerable legacy.

CHAPTER 14

RENÉ GOSCINNY

THE MULTITALENTED, MULTINATIONAL
RENÉ GOSCINNY WAS SHAPED BY LIFE IN SEVERAL
OF THE WORLD'S MAJOR CITIES AND GREW TO
COCREATE ONE OF THE MOST POPULAR COMIC
BOOKS IN ALL OF FRANCE AND AROUND
THE GLOBE.

Born in Paris to Jewish immigrant parents from Poland, raised in Buenos Aires, Argentina, relocated to New York, and then finally ending up back in Paris, René Goscinny was brought up in a whirlwind international lifestyle. His lifetime of around-the-world influences and a deep sense of the history of many countries enriched the French character of his most famous creations.

While he worked in the famous New York City advertising industry in 1948, the young Goscinny shared a studio with the cartoonists Jack Davis, Will Elder, and Harvey Kurtzman; all three would help launch *Mad* at EC Comics and revolutionize cartooning. It was here, surrounded by these enormous talents, that Goscinny fell in love with comic books.

Albert Uderzo

After returning to Paris, Goscinny met the cartoonist Albert Uderzo in 1951, and for nearly 10 years they collaborated on comics and strips, including contributions to the magazine *Tintin*. During this time, he also worked with the cartoonist Jean-Jacques Sempé on the beloved *Le Petit Nicolas* (*Little Nicolas*), beginning in 1956. Goscinny wrote comic strips and prose stories about the life of a clever, fun-loving, occasionally mischievous French boy, going to school, playing with his friends, and dealing with the baffling world of grownups. *Le Petit Nicolas* books were adapted into English- and Spanish-language editions,

Jean-Jacques Sempé

as well as made into a movie and an animated series in 2009, and another movie in 2014.

In the years shortly after publishing the earliest Nicolas strips, Goscinny partnered with Uderzo and other writers and cartoonists. They cofounded the Edipress/Edifrance syndicate, publishing comics for corporate clients. In 1959, the same year as the first Petit Nicolas prose book, Goscinny and his partners launched a magazine—*Pilote*—and now needed comics to fill it.

Pilote was where Goscinny published his most famous cocreation, *Asterix*, with Uderzo drawing. These were the comedic adventures of a Gaul—a native of a region of ancient Europe that overlaps with modern-day France and its neighboring countries—who lived over two thousand years ago. When their village is menaced by the Roman Empire, Panoramix, a druid, concocts a potion for super strength. Drinking it, Asterix and his friend Obelix defend the village from invasion, as well as travel and have adventures all over the world.

Asterix is one of the most popular comic books in the history of France and a lifelong favorite of kids growing up all over Europe; it is still in publication today. Asterix and Obelix endure as two of the most popular comic book characters in the world. So great is the popularity of Asterix that the comic has been translated into over a hundred languages and has formed the basis of four live-action movies and thirteen animated movies. There's even a theme park outside Paris, called Parc Astérix.

Another of Goscinny's partners was the cartoonist Jean Tabary. In 1962, the two started publishing a series in the comics magazine Record, before bringing it home to their own Pilote in 1968— the misadventures of the crooked Iznogoud, an ambitious and power-hungry grand vizier of ancient Baghdad, in what is today Iraq. Starting out as a supporting character in the strip Les aventures du Calife Haroun el Poussah, Iznogoud—who takes his name from the pun that "he's no good"—is the second-in-command to the caliph, the ruler of Baghdad, and aspires to depose him and take his position. Iznogoud was greedy and villainous, but he became such a beloved and popular character that Goscinny and Tabary made him the star and renamed the strip Iznogoud.

Goscinny died of a heart attack at the all-too-young age of 51. Uderzo carried on Asterix by himself until handing it off to other cartoonists.

One of Le Petit Nicolas's most famous, best-loved stories is the one about Nicolas staying home sick from school. The boy sits up in bed in his pajamas, resting his head on a giant pillow, surrounded by comics books…with a huge smile on his face! This is truly one of the best ways to celebrate Goscinny's remarkable life and work.

CHAPTER 15

RUMIKO TAKAHASHI

FROM HER START AS A FAN SELLING HER OWN SELF-PUBLISHED MANGA AT CONVENTIONS TO BECOMING ONE OF THE MOST CELEBRATED COMIC BOOK CREATORS IN THE WORLD, THE JOURNEY OF RUMIKO TAKAHASHI IS AS ASTONISHING AS THE ADVENTURES OF HER COLORFUL CHARACTERS.

The Angoulême International Comics Festival in France is Europe's second largest comic book event—and the third largest in the world behind only Japan's Comiket and Italy's Lucca Comics & Games—and without a doubt one of the most prestigious. In 2019, a voting pool of 1,700 cartoonists selected Rumiko Takahashi, the legendary creator of *Ranma ½*, *Urusei Yatsura*, and *Inuyasha*, to win the festival's top prize, the Grand Prix. This was an incredible honor for someone who started out attending conventions like the aforementioned Comiket to sell and trade her own self-published comics.

Takahashi, born in 1957 in the city of Niigata, Japan, was a young university student who dreamed of making manga. She studied

Takahashi studying with Kazuo Koike

under the writer Kazuo Koike at his own manga school, Gekiga Sonjuku, where in 1975 she began producing *dōjinshi*——fan-made manga, self-published or even just photocopied to sell and trade with other fans. Koike was the acclaimed writer, famous even then, of *Kozure Ōkami* (*Lone Wolf and Cub*), with artist Goseki Kojima, and *Shirayuka hime* (*Lady Snowblood*) with Kazuo Kamimura, among other series. *Lady Snowblood* had been serialized from 1972 to 1973, while *Lone Wolf and Cub*, launched in 1970, was still ongoing. Koike had written the screenplays for film

Dōjinshi is fan-made manga

adaptations of both; in short, the writer was a sensation, and to train with him was a valuable opportunity.

Japan's manga culture is extremely welcoming toward dōjinshi—even turning a blind eye to copyright issues when fans create manga about existing properties—which creates fertile ground for talented, undiscovered young creators to build a fan base. And with a huge market of magazines publishing manga on a weekly basis, publishers continuously need new material to fill their pages, creating plenty of opportunities for those creators to get noticed and break in.

After a few years creating a handful of dōjinshi, Takahashi began working in 1978 with the publisher Shogakukan, which gave her a shot at the young age of 20 with her one-off short comedic story *Katte na Yatsura* (*Those Selfish Aliens*). Within the same year, Shogakukan began publishing Takahashi's first serial in its magazine *Weekly Shōnen Sunday*—an expanded new take on her previous alien short, called *Urusei Yatsura*. Sometimes also called *Lum* in English, it was the humorous science fiction story of the alien princess Lum who falls in love with a hapless young creep, Ataru Moroboshi; he beats her at a game of tag, and she mistakenly thinks it means they are engaged to be married and moves in with him.

Urusei Yatsura was not an instant hit, but it impressed the publisher enough to let the serial go on beyond the initial plan of just five chapters, eventually running for 374 chapters and nearly 6,000 pages. It first found success a year into its initial run, and it endures today as Takahashi's first major work and one of her all-time best. The manga was adapted into a TV series, and four movies were released in theaters.

In 1980, while working on *Urusei Yatsura*, Takahashi began serializing *Mezon Ikkoku* (*Maison Ikkoku*), about the romantic misadventures of neighbors at a boarding house, in another weekly Shogakukan magazine, *Big Comic Spirits*. *Maison Ikkoku* ran for 15 volumes and was adapted as an animated series, a live-action movie, and live-action TV specials, becoming Takahashi's second success and firmly establishing her as a major manga star well before both series ended in 1987.

Takahashi's next feat led to the creation of one of the first anime series to become popular in the United States: beginning in 1987, she started publishing *Ranma Nibun-no-Ichi* (*Ranma ½*) in *Weekly Shōnen Sunday*. Takahashi's work already displayed her predilection for casts of characters with rich inner lives and webs of complex relationships between them, and in *Ranma ½* (pronounced *Ranma One-Half*), that talent rose to new heights.

It told the story of the teen martial artist Ranma and his father, Genma, the owner of a dojo, who fall into a cursed spring and are transformed. Every time Ranma and Genma are doused with cold water, Ranma changes into a young woman, and Genma into a panda. Only hot water changes them back. Genma's plan of an arranged marriage for Ranma becomes complicated by both of their transformations, and Ranma juggles pursuing the women he wants to date while becoming the unwitting object of other men's affections. Like much of Takahashi's work, *Ranma* combined action with romantic comedy and fantastical elements, and historians have pointed to it as a major inspiration on most of the work to follow in those genres.

Ranma was published weekly for 9 years, filling 407 chapters, and collected in 38 book-length volumes. The end of the serialized run in 1996 was marked with the release of *The Ranma ½ Memorial Book*, featuring art, an interview with Takahashi, and other bonus content. The manga was translated to English and released in the U.S. as a monthly comic book, as well as being adapted into 2 anime series, 11 OVAs (original video animation releases), 3 movies, a live-action TV movie, and 15 video games.

Takahashi took a darker approach toward her next major work, *Inuyasha*, serialized from 1996 to 2008. It told the story of 15-year-old Kagome Higurashi, who finds herself transported to 16th-century Japan, where she teams up with Inuyasha, a dog-man *yōkai* (a supernatural creature or demon), to collect the powerful shards of a shattered jewel before the demon Naraku does. It became the basis for two anime series running more than 200 total episodes, an OVA, and four movies.

These were only four of the most prominent of Takahashi's many series over her 40-year career, selling approximately 200 million books total. Takahashi is considered one of the most influential manga creators of all time, and even in the West she's received many awards and has been inducted into the Eisner Hall of Fame. The cartoonist Bryan Lee O'Malley cited *Ranma ½* as a particular influence on his *Scott Pilgrim* series of comics, which were adapted as the 2010 movie *Scott Pilgrim vs. the World.*

In early 2019, the news was announced that Takahashi would be awarded the Grand Prix at Angoulême, a lifetime achievement award honoring a career full of distinction. Previous winners include Will Eisner, the great French comic book creator Moebius (a.k.a. Jean Giraud), and *Calvin and Hobbes* cartoonist Bill Watterson. Takahashi was only the second woman to win the Grand Prix at Angoulême after the French cartoonist Florence Cestac, and only the second Japanese creator to win after Katsuhiro Otomo, author of the manga masterpiece *Akira.*

CHAPTER 16

HÉCTOR GERMÁN OESTERHELD

IN A TIME OF TYRANNY IN ARGENTINA, THE POINTED WORK OF THE COMIC BOOK WRITER HÉCTOR GERMÁN OESTERHELD REPRESENTED A MENACE TO THE COUNTRY'S LEADERS. HIS ULTIMATE FATE WAS A TESTAMENT TO THE GREAT PERSUASIVE POWER OF COMICS.

The South American nation of Argentina, one of the ten largest countries in the world, boasts rich traditions in art, literature, music, cuisine, architecture, film, sports, and more. It was the birthplace of tango and the home country of Pope Francis, and it has produced countless luminaries, including the rock star Gustavo Cerati, the *fútbol* player Lionel Messi, and one of the world's all-time great authors, Jorge Luis Borges.

Despite its tremendous cultural heritage, however, Argentina suffered through decades of turbulent political upheaval for most of the 20th century. The country began the century under an ironclad hegemony, with one party manipulating politics to hold power indefinitely. The 1916 election restored self-determination to the voting public, but a decades-long series of takeovers and revolutions beginning in 1930 saw control of the country shift back and forth between military dictatorships and civilian governments. By the early 1970s, with the government ruled by a *junta*—a group of self-installed military leaders—subversives worked to under-mine the state's forces of terror through guerrilla tactics including kidnapping and sabotage. Elections were held in 1973 to calm the turmoil, and former president Juan Perón was allowed to return from exile. Perón's followers had been separating into a conser-vative, pro-military right-wing movement and a leftist, pro-labor movement fighting state terror. When Perón greeted a crowd of two million at the airport, the split tore wide open—a group of his far-right supporters fired machine guns into the crowd, targeting his left-wing supporters; they killed at least a dozen people and injured hundreds. This led to Argentina's darkest period: the Dirty War. Enter Héctor Germán Oesterheld.

Born in Buenos Aires in 1919, Oesterheld was a journalist, reporting in the newspaper *La Prensa*. In the late 1940s and early '50s,

Hugo Pratt

he began to make friends with Italian comic book creators who had moved to Argentina, including the great Hugo Pratt, who would later publish one of Italy's finest comics, *Corto Maltese*, about the adventures of an intrepid sea captain. Oesterheld started writing comics, helping kick off "the Golden Age of Argentine Comics" (*la Época de oro de la historieta argentina*). For the next decade, Oesterheld, the artists Alberto Breccia and Francisco Solano López, the cartoonist Quino (Joaquín Salvador Lavado, creator of *Mafalda*), and many others released the most important comics in the country's history.

Oesterheld founded a publisher, Editorial Frontera, in 1957 and launched several comic book magazines, including weekly and monthly editions of *Hora Cero*. Oesterheld and Solano López created a series there together, *El Eternauta* (*The Eternaut*), a sci-fi tale of the time-traveling survivor of an apocalyptic climate event and alien invasion. Wearing a homemade biohazard suit to survive the poisonous snowfall, Juan Salvo (the would-be *eternaut*, a traveler through eternity) fights alien creatures and works to uncover the shadowy figures who control everything. He ends up lost in

Francisco Solano López

time, searching for his family. Oesterheld and Solano López published *El Eternauta* weekly for 106 chapters from 1957 to 1959, and rebooted it in 1969 with heavier political overtones, using fiction and metaphor to criticize the junta. A sequel followed in 1976. *El Eternauta* is considered one of the finest comics to come out of Argentina, as well as one of the strongest works of science fiction. Fantagraphics Books released a translated edition in 2015, the first time this monumental work was made available in English.

One of Argentina's most outstanding comic book artists was Alberto Breccia who, with Oesterheld, cocreated *Mort Cinder* in 1962 in the magazine *Misterix*. The title character of Mort Cinder was a sort of immortal, returning to life every time he died, who had been on Earth since antiquity. Having witnessed many of the feats and follies of civilization, Cinder had a great understanding of the human capacity for good and evil and took a dim view of it all.

In 1966, a new coup d'etat—a violent military takeover of the government—led to widespread censorship and an economic downturn. Editorial Frontera went out of business, and Oesterheld started to make his comic books more explicitly political. He reteamed with Breccia, and Breccia's son Enrique, in 1968 for a comic book biography—*Che: Vida de Ernesto Che Guevara*—about Che Guevara, the Argentine-born doctor, author,

Alberto and Enrique Breccia

and freedom fighter who aided in Fidel Castro's Cuban Revolution. Argentina banned the book, ordering the destruction of all copies and of the printing plates used to publish it. Fearing for their safety, the Breccias hid or destroyed their original hand-drawn pages; they burned some, buried others in the ground, and entrusted a small number to friends outside the country. Few copies of the book are known to still exist.

Juan Perón took power in 1973 but died the year after; leadership fell to his wife Isabel. The country was undergoing economic collapse, and insurgent activity against the government was widespread, leading to yet another military takeover in 1976, deposing Isabel Perón and installing a new junta. This time, Argentina's brutal military dictatorship had the support of the United States government. It was an era of state-sponsored terrorism and crimes against humanity called the Dirty War. For the sake of America's economic interests in Latin America, the U.S. preferred a capitalist junta, no matter how despotic, to the socialist movement that might win elections if allowed to exist.

In 1976, Oesterheld wrote his pointedly critical *Eternauta* sequel in the magazine *Skorpio*. *El Eternauta, parte II* depicted a version of Argentina suffering under a brutal dictatorship, not unlike the regime that had just taken power. After that, Oesterheld and his daughters "disappeared."

A favored tactic of the government during this time was what came to be known as making people "disappear"; anyone deemed a threat would be seized from their home in the night, never to be seen or heard from again, with no record of their arrest. Citizens were abducted, taken to secret prisons, tortured, killed, and buried in unmarked graves. Others were dropped, alive, out of an airplane flying over the sea. These victims are called *los desaparecidos* ("the disappeared" or "the missing"); it's believed that as many as 30,000 people met these fates.

Oesterheld disappeared in 1976, and the following year his four daughters, ranging in age from 18 to 25, were arrested, as well as their husbands. Oesterheld's wife, Elsa, was able to remain free. Elsa Sánchez became one of the women to take part in the *Madres de Plaza de Mayo* demonstrations, held by an organization of mothers (the Mothers of Plaza de Mayo) denouncing the disappearance of their families. One of Oesterheld's daughters had a son, Martín, while in custody. Elsa was able to recover him from the government years later.

The Italian writer Alberto Ongaro claims he was told the reason for Oesterheld's disappearance: "We did away with him because he wrote the most beautiful story of Che Guevara ever done." Poetic embellishment, probably, but the statement speaks to the truth of Héctor Oesterheld's death: he was murdered because he wielded power enough to threaten a dictatorship with comic books.

CHAPTER 17

LOUISE SIMONSON

"WEEZIE," AS SHE'S KNOWN TO FRIENDS AND LOVED ONES, BEGAN HER CAREER EDITING HORROR COMICS FOR WARREN PUBLISHING AND SUPERHEROES FOR MARVEL, BEFORE QUITTING HER JOB TO WRITE FULL-TIME. BUT THE RELATIVELY UNKNOWN SIMONSON COCREATED SOME SERIOUSLY WELL-KNOWN HEROES AND VILLAINS AND DESERVES A BIG SPOTLIGHT.

The young Mary Louise Alexander——going by the professional name of Louise Jones, using her ex-husband's last name—began her editorial career in the magazine industry, already enjoying friendships with cartoonists and comic book creators. She modeled for the acclaimed horror cartoonist Bernie Wrightson, who featured her on the cover of *House of Secrets* #92, the first comic to feature his famed cocreation, Swamp Thing. In 1974, Louise Jones joined Warren Publishing as an assistant editor.

Jones's six-year career at Warren was distinguished; she rose to the level of senior editor, overseeing all the company's magazines of horror comics. By the end of the 1970s, Jones left Warren, and in 1980, she married the cartoonist Walt Simonson and took his name. As Louise Simonson, she entered the best-known phase of her career and began the comic book work she still carries on today.

Initially, Simonson joined Marvel and became the editor of such legendary comic books as *Star Wars*, *Indiana Jones*, and *Uncanny X-Men*. The X-Men comic was such a smash hit at the time that Marvel demanded a spin-off series; under Simonson's oversight, *Uncanny X-Men* writer Chris Claremont and the artist Bob McLeod cocreated *New Mutants*, the adventures of a band of the younger students at Professor X's mutant academy. McLeod left the series almost immediately after launching, and the art was briefly taken over by Sal Buscema; but the comic truly reached its pinnacle in issue #18, with a new full-time artist: Bill Sienkiewicz. *New Mutants* was a groundbreaking work—dark, violent, and chilling—still revered today by fans and the countless comic book artists and writers who were influenced by it.

As dark as *New Mutants* was, Simonson had sunnier visions as well, like her idea of an all-child super team. During the 1980s, Marvel had editors writing comics for the company, though Simonson didn't subscribe to that policy; she preferred to share the work with freelance writers. But when her editing workload shrank and she had time on her hands, Simonson pitched her idea to Marvel and took on her first writing assignment. She and the artist June Brigman teamed up to cocreate *Power Pack*; it was the story of the Power family, four brothers and sisters ranging in age from 12 down to 5, who were given special powers by a benevolent alien seeking to help Earth. *Power Pack* was a beloved, long-lasting comic book series; it featured young heroes and appealed to young readers, without shying away from tense dramatic situations, like the kids debating (and never agreeing) whether it was right to keep their powers a secret from their parents, teachers, and friends.

Still not content to juggle writing and editing duties, Simonson quit her job at Marvel to go into writing full-time. When Marvel wanted yet another *X-Men* spin-off, Simonson lobbied to get the assignment, with a list of pitch ideas for *X-Factor*. Simonson got the job in 1986; in her very first issue, she and the artist Jackson Guice cocreated the villain Apocalypse, the world's oldest mutant and one of the X-Men's most powerful enemies to this day. In

1987, Simonson took over the writing on her old editorial beat, *New Mutants*, and found herself in a position to help create a major new character. In a convoluted brainstorming process between Simonson, Marvel's editor in chief Bob Harras, the artist and coplotter Rob Liefeld, and others, the team unveiled an extreme, gun-toting new antihero: Cable.

Simonson, Liefeld, and Harras

Simonson branched out and started writing for DC Comics in 1991, where she helped launch a new monthly Superman series, *Superman: The Man of Steel*. During the landmark "Death of Superman" storyline, unfolding across the four monthly Superman comics, Simonson and the artist Jon Bogdanove cocreated Steel in 1993, introducing a beloved character that endures today. Steel was John Henry Irons, an armor-wearing, hammer-wielding, African American hero, one of four would-be Superman replacements who took up the charge when the Man of Steel seemed to die fighting the monstrous villain Doomsday. After the event, DC gave Steel his own comic book, which Simonson wrote for 31 issues.

Louise Simonson's legacy is far bigger than the recognition she's gotten. She still writes comics today…but not nearly enough!

CHAPTER 18

KELLY SUE DECONNICK

HIGHER. FURTHER. FASTER. MORE.
FROM OBSCURE WORK RESCRIPTING MANGA
TRANSLATIONS AND WRITING HORROR COMICS, TO
WALKING THE RED CARPET AT A HOLLYWOOD
MOVIE PREMIERE, KELLY SUE DECONNICK'S RISE
WAS AS METEORIC AS THE FAMOUS FLYING
SUPERHERO SHE WROTE—CAPTAIN MARVEL.

Kelly Sue DeConnick grew up flying.

Born in Ohio in 1970, DeConnick's father was in the U.S. Air Force, and the future writer moved from base to base with her family. One constant was comic books, readily available at every air base general store.

DeConnick came to the attention of Marvel in 2010, where she proved her talent writing two one-shot adventures: *Rescue*, with artist Andrea Mutti, about the superhero Pepper Potts becomes when she dons her own model of Tony Stark's Iron armor, and *Sif*, with art by Ryan Stegman, a story of Asgard's greatest female warrior confronting her tormentor, Loki.

But where DeConnick really broke out was with *Osborn* the following year—a dark, often shocking miniseries with artist Emma Ríos that followed Norman Osborn, the former Green Goblin, as he is incarcerated in a top-secret prison for supervillains. *Osborn* was a comic with no good guys and no redemption; the bad guys rebel against their illegal, unethical imprisonment, and the forces of law and order bend the rules and compromise their morality for what they believe to be a greater good. DeConnick would follow up *Osborn* with something much sunnier.

Mar-Vell, a soldier of an alien race, the Kree, fought in his people's centuries-long war against the shape-shifting Skrulls. After coming to Earth undercover as an Air Force officer, Mar-Vell uses his alien abilities for good as a superhero, calling himself Captain Marvel.

Andrea Mutti   **Emma Ríos**   **Jamie McKelvie**

Carol Danvers, his friend and fellow Air Force officer, is exposed to Mar-Vell's powers and becomes Ms. Marvel. She bases her initial costume—a skimpy leotard with her stomach exposed, accessorized with a pilot's scarf—after Captain Marvel's Kree uniform and becomes his protégé. But Mar-Vell's story ended in 1982, in the graphic novel *The Death of Captain Marvel*, when the alien hero falls ill and dies in an all-too-human way.

DeConnick and editor Stephen Wacker agreed in 2012 that it was time for *Ms.* Marvel to become *Captain* Marvel. The artist Jamie McKelvie designed her new look, combining three influences: the style and colors from Mar-Vell's and Ms. Marvel's original Kree uniforms, the sash around the waist from Carol's most recent costume, and the look of a pilot's flight suit…and Carol Danvers became Captain Marvel!

The influence of DeConnick's Air Force upbringing was clear; Captain Marvel is a fighter pilot and superhero who vows to "punch a hole in the sky." Kelly Sue DeConnick's take on Carol Danvers, combined with the McKelvie costume, became instantly iconic, suddenly establishing an all-new standard for this decades-old character and inspiring the 2019 movie.

After blazing a path through mainstream American superhero comics, DeConnick and her beloved *Osborn* collaborator, Emma Ríos—the two call each other "sister kraken," after the mythical sea monster—banded together and created their own series, *Pretty Deadly*, about the daughter of Death himself, called Deathface Ginny. Unfolding as a fairy tale that a rabbit tells to a butterfly, one volume was set in the Old West, another in the trenches of World War I. Shortly after, DeConnick teamed with the artist Valentine De Landro to create an uncompromising science fiction comic set in space, inspired by the "women in prison" genre of schlocky 1970s movies. *Bitch Planet* takes its title from the nickname given to a space station where women are jailed for being "non-compliant" in a sexist society of the future. The comic book's insignia for its non-compliant prisoners, "NC," was instantly embraced by DeConnick's legions of fans, using t-shirts and tattoos to brand themselves with the letters proudly and defiantly.

After dedicating years to her own independent creations, Kelly Sue DeConnick made a highly acclaimed return to superheroes, signing up with DC Comics to write Aquaman. Nothing seemed further from the high-flying Captain Marvel than the deep-sea Aquaman…but both characters spent decades as lesser-known also-rans before becoming sudden sensations and movie stars. DeConnick's skill at uncovering humble humanity and powerful grandeur consistently brings out the best in the characters she writes.

CHAPTER 19

RIUS

FOR A MAN WHO ACTUALLY TRIED TO MAKE ENEMIES, RIUS WAS WILDLY SUCCESSFUL. THE FAMED MEXICAN CARTOONIST USED HIS COMICS TO ATTACK THE ABUSES OF BIG BUSINESS, THE GOVERNMENT, AND THE CATHOLIC CHURCH...AND THEY HATED HIM FOR IT.

Eduardo del Río, born in 1934 in the city of Zamora in the Mexican state of Michoacán, attended seminary and trained to become a Catholic priest. Things didn't quite work out that way…del Río took the pen name Rius and turned his razor-sharp pen against the Catholic Church and other institutions, as one of Mexico's most relentless social critics and most beloved cartoonists.

Rius published over 100 books in his lifetime, specializing in nonfiction comics about social commentary and satire. A fierce critic of the Mexican and U.S. governments, Rius championed the Cuban Revolution, led by Fidel Castro, in his 1966 book *Cuba para principiantes* (*Cuba for Beginners*). He followed that up in 1970 with *Marx para principiantes* (*Marx for Beginners*), an anticapitalist statement in praise of Karl Marx, the socialist revolutionary and author of *The Communist Manifesto*.

These two *para principiantes* volumes and others by Rius were so popular and influential, they kicked off a trend of comic books and graphic novels by many different authors titled "*…for Beginners*" and "*Introducing…*" throughout the 1980s, '90s, and 2000s. Sometimes these books covered subjects as innocuous and educational as *Einstein for Beginners* and *Introducing Newton*; other times they used the medium of comics to tackle complicated, baffling topics like *Introducing Quantum Theory* and *Chaos for Beginners*; but mostly, following Rius's example, these comics provided readers with a progressive take on issues such as *Black History for Beginners* and *Introducing Feminism*.

Rius's most famous and successful works by far were his two ongoing comic book series: in 1965, he began writing and drawing *Los Supermachos,* published by Editorial Meridiano. *Los Supermachos* was set in a fictional small, impoverished town, home to an uncommonly wise and well-informed central character, Juan Calzónzin, whose opinions and viewpoints provided commentary on Mexican society and the world at large. Ironically, *Los Supermachos* was so successful for Meridiano that they took it from Rius and continued to publish volumes by other authors. To take its place, Rius created *Los Agachados* in 1968 (*The Crouched Ones*) and continued publishing new stories for 13 years. It followed a large cast of working-class characters who remarked on every aspect of modern life, from heady topics like politics and religion to more light-hearted preoccupations like music and sports, and everything in between. Rius may have named this comic in homage to the working-class subjects of a landmark Mexican artwork: Manuel Álvarez Bravo's famous 1934 photo titled *Los Agachados*, which featured a row of hard-working men on their break at a lunch counter. Neither Álvarez Bravo's subjects nor Rius's comic book characters do a lot of crouching, as their titles imply; rather, both works refer to crouching as a symbol for life in the working class, where people struggle and get by under the overpowering might of the world's power structures.

In 1969, Rius was apprehended by the police and turned over to the military. According to Rius's telling—in a story that he may or may not have embellished—they accused him of being an enemy of the state over his comics, marched him to an open grave, and threatened to kill him…only to free him when the soldiers realized he was related to a former Mexican president and his disappearance was likely to be investigated.

Rius published *El manual del perfecto ateo* in 1980 (*The Handbook of the Perfect Atheist*), a work of antireligious satire. The Church found the comic book so offensive that it excommunicated him—an extreme measure to expel a person from the institution, usually reserved for the perpetrators of the vilest crimes against the faith. From then on, Rius—who, at one time, had planned on becoming a priest—was no longer a member in good standing of the Catholic Church.

Although Rius's comics were vulgar and spiteful, fans and commentators characterize his work—and him—as extremely intelligent and incisive. While his work may have been considered provocative, reactionary, and angry, even his detractors agree that Rius delivered valid critiques of the problems of society and its unjust power structures.

Rius died in 2017 at the age of 83. He believed comics and humor, because they're entertaining and funny, are more effective communication than philosophy and prose. The targets of his criticism—who tried to do everything in their power to silence him—seemed to agree.

CHAPTER 20

KATSUHIRO OTOMO

AT THE DAWN OF OUR DIGITAL AGE, THE "CYBERPUNK" SCIENCE FICTION MANGA OF KATSUHIRO OTOMO—AND HIS CONTEMPORARIES SHIROW MASAMUNE AND YUKITO KISHIRO—FORESAW THE PROMISE AND PERIL HUMANITY HAD IN STORE.

As the 1980s wore on and the '90s approached, technology felt like it was approaching a major turning point. In more and more households around the world, broadcast television was being replaced by high-speed digital cable with dozens of channels; personal computers were becoming a staple, with sophisticated software and even modems; and rotary telephones had given way to push-button touch-tone phones, which were now being replaced by cordless models—some people had even started using cell phones. There was this thing called the internet; magazine articles were excited to predict that someday we'd do all our shopping there. Taken together, all these streams of communication were nicknamed the information superhighway.

It definitely sounds corny in hindsight. But if you can possibly imagine, the onset of digital technology represented a seismic shift for human society. Before computers and smartphones took us online, the technology we lived with every day had basically stayed the same for half a century. Whether it had a rotary dial or buttons, a telephone was a telephone; a color TV worked the same way as a black-and-white TV.

But digital technology required our brains to take a leap just to understand it. Video games introduced the novel idea of controlling an animated character on your TV; such a thing had never been remotely possible. Now there were portable telephones, and people were making new friends on the internet? Try explaining that to your great-grandparents. What was next, a computer wristwatch?

A select few visionaries understood these trends for what they promised: profound human transformation. Conservative governments came into power in the United States, United Kingdom, and elsewhere, and the influence of consumer corporations like Coca-Cola and McDonald's was growing. A new kind of sci-fi emerged, imagining our interaction with the new world around us, mixing technological terror with satire of our new commercial existence—cyberpunk.

In Japan, the cyberpunk movement began in 1982 with one groundbreaking manga: *Akira* by Katsuhiro Otomo. However, a snapshot of Japanese cyberpunk would be woefully incomplete without two other landmark works of the era: Shirow Masamune's *The Ghost in the Shell*, and *Battle Angel Alita* by Yukito Kishiro.

Katsuhiro Otomo's *Akira*—only his second major work—ran for eight years in *Shūkan Yangu Magajin* (*Weekly Young Magazine*), and its impact on manga,

Japan

Japanese culture, and global science fiction would turn out to be as enormous as the explosion in its opening pages. Serialized from 1982 to 1990, the story is set in the near-future year of 2019; it follows multiple protagonists after a single incident brings their diverse lives together. In the years after an unexplained atomic blast destroyed Tokyo and started World War III, the city is rebuilt as Neo Tokyo and is set to host the Olympic Games. But civil unrest is widespread, antigovernment rebels fight the military with guerrilla tactics, and roving motorcycle gangs of teenage delinquents battle on the expressway. The story begins when a mysterious apparition causes these groups to crash together— almost literally. A gang of bikers led by Kaneda sees a ghostly child with white hair and elderly features on the expressway in front of them. One of the bikers, Tetsuo (Kaneda's best frenemy), crashes explosively into a psychic force field, and the elderly-looking child disappears. The military takes Tetsuo away for study, as the incident awakens his psychic powers. Kaneda tries to follow, crossing paths with rebels who had stolen away the boy from a government facility in the first place. Eventually, we learn that a top-secret government program has been cultivating psychic powers in a handful of children for decades. The most powerful of these is a boy named Akira, and the outburst of his power was the explosion that destroyed Tokyo, not an atomic blast. Akira has been kept in suspended animation deep underground ever since, but the introduction of Tetsuo into the mix threatens to reawaken him and unleash destruction. In light of the profound technological transformation of the era, *Akira* is the story of human beings pushed to cross the next evolutionary milestone and become something more than human, and of ordinary people with everyday lives struggling to find their place as the world changes all around them.

Otomo cowrote and personally directed an *Akira* feature film in 1988, while the series was still being published. Drastically abridging the manga's 2,000 pages into a convoluted, two-hour plot was no small feat. Nevertheless, the movie was a masterpiece and a massive hit. *Akira* broke with the standards of hyperefficient animation established by Osamu Tezuka and *Astro Boy*, opting instead for hand-painted backgrounds, fully animated figures, and a richly immersive world. It was the most expensive anime film ever made at the time, and it set the standard for a new generation of formally ambitious animated movies to follow.

In the realm of cyberpunk, two other masterpieces made a comparable mark: Shirow Masamune's *Kokaku Kidotai* (literally *Mobile Armored Riot Police*, but published in English with the title *The Ghost in the Shell*) and Yukito Kishiro's *Ganmu* (literally *Gun Dream*, but retitled *Battle Angel Alita*) both depicted worlds where cybernetic bodily enhancements are common. In *Ghost in the Shell*, which ran from 1989 to 1990, Major Motoko Kusanagi—a blue-haired supercop with a fully robotic body—leads a specialized task force, Public Security Section 9. Their team specializes in cyber-crime and international intrigue, catching hackers and digital saboteurs. Kusanagi chases down threats online with the computer in her brain, but she also fights real-world foes with her fists and high-tech guns.

Battle Angel Alita was published from 1990 to 1995. With faint echoes of *Astro Boy*, it is the story of a powerful robot adopted by a kind scientist. Doctor Ido finds a discarded robot's torso and head in the trash, which he names Alita; although she doesn't appear to be functioning, her human brain is intact, so he repairs her body and Alita lives, with no memory of her past. The story is set in a city known only as Scrapyard, existing under the shadow of a massive airborne nation, Zalem. It is a hardscrabble existence full of thieves, killers, and bounty hunters, and when Alita discovers she has mastery of the robotic martial art called panzerkunst, she becomes a bounty hunter, though it is only the start of her lifelong journey of self-discovery.

Battle Angel stands out for the psychological richness of its characters, especially Alita. Over the course of nine collected volumes, she matures from an impulsive girl with the mentality of a teenager, smitten with the first trashy boy she has a crush on, into a wise woman who reflects on the lessons of her experiences. Kishiro, who began his career drawing manga at age 17, cites Rumiko Takahashi as an influence on his work; no surprise considering the emotional depth.

The worlds of *Akira*, *Battle Angel Alita*, and *Ghost in the Shell* possess remarkable technology, but the people who live in them are no happier or any more advanced than we are; rather, they're moving stories of human drama in the midst of dizzying transformation.

CHAPTER 21

WENDY AND
RICHARD PINI

THIS HUSBAND-AND-WIFE TEAM BEGAN
PUBLISHING *ELFQUEST* AT A TURNING POINT IN THE
COMIC BOOK INDUSTRY: THE DIRECT MARKET.
THE BIRTH OF COMIC BOOK SHOPS ALLOWED
WENDY AND RICHARD PINI TO EXTEND THEIR
FANTASY-ADVENTURE SERIES INTO A
40-YEAR EPIC.

During the era of "Bullpen Bulletins," the clubhouse-like editorial pages at the back of Marvel comic books, Stan Lee ran reader mail including the letter writers' full names and addresses. It would be unwise to give away people's personal information that way today, but in the 1960s, it opened a path for people to correspond with each other after their letters saw print. (That's how you would have found the Bayonne, New Jersey, home address of 15-year-old George R.R. Martin, the future *Game of Thrones* author, in his fan letter to *Fantastic Four*.)

The Silver Surfer #5, written by Lee and drawn by the great John Buscema in 1968, featured fan mail by 17-year-old Wendy Fletcher. Richard Pini, 18 years old, read it and sent her a letter, and the two teens began writing to each other. Ten years later, married, they would go on to cocreate *Elfquest*, an epic comic book fantasy that ran for 40 years.

Growing up in California, Wendy Fletcher idolized Jack Kirby and Osamu Tezuka, and she drew inspiration from many sources, including Arthur Rackham, the British artist known for his depictions of fantasy and fairy tales. Her passion for these influences led her to become a science fiction and fantasy artist, illustrating covers of books and magazines; she was also a fixture at comic book conventions, exhibiting art and attending in costume as the sword-fighting warrior Red Sonja. Richard Pini, of Connecticut, was a science fiction fan who studied astronomy at MIT, where he became a comic book reader and discovered Fletcher's letter. After college, he went to work at the Charles Hayden Planetarium in Boston and taught astronomy in high school.

Richard and Wendy married in 1972; in 1977, they founded their own start-up publisher, combining the first letters of the phrase "Wendy and Richard Pini" to call it WaRP Graphics. In 1978, they began self-publishing *Elfquest*, a 20-issue series set in a fantasy world where humans coexist with various tribes of elves descended from alien settlers. Cutter, chief of the Wolfrider tribe, sets out on the titular quest to find others of his kind all over the World of Two Moons. (Chapter 1 appeared in the magazine *Fantasy Quarterly* on February 28, 1978, but the Pinis took up self-publishing through WaRP with issue #2.)

From the birth of comic books in the 1930s until the 1970s, comic books were sold primarily on newsstands and at convenience stores, candy shops, and any other business that cared to carry them. This distribution system favored comics as a cheap, disposable commodity, as they were in their early years; comic books in a pharmacy or supermarket checkout line would cost only cents (anywhere from five cents to prices nearing a dollar, depending on the era) and were stuffed into spinning displays and other wire racks, causing them to flop forward and develop creases, which was perfectly fine for something you were sticking in your pocket and trading with a friend or throwing away after reading. And because most comic books featured a self-contained, one-part story, a fan who couldn't find an issue due to spotty distribution or depleted inventory wasn't missing anything crucial. But in the '60s, when Marvel started courting older readers and telling multipart serials like the Galactus storyline in *Fantastic Four* #48 to #50, making sure to get every issue became essential to fans, who also collected old issues with care.

A few specialty comic book stores started to pop up in the 1960s, but the '70s was when the phenomenon of the "direct market" fully emerged. Drugstores and supermarkets (what was termed the "newsstand market") ordered any amount of a comic book they wanted—say, 100 copies—and then could rip off the covers of any copies that didn't sell and mail those back to the distributor as "unsold inventory" to get their money back. To supply this inventory, publishers would take a chance on printing hundreds of thousands, even millions of copies of a comic book and cross their fingers that it sold and they wouldn't have to refund stores for what didn't.

In the new direct market, stores specializing in comics and other entertainment ordered directly from publishers (although distributors would enter the picture later to handle the selling and shipping). If the owner of a comic shop had 50 customers lined up to buy the next issue of *Amazing Spider-Man*, she might order 75 from Marvel—50 to fulfill the sure-fire demand and another 25 to keep on the shelf for walk-in customers. The trade-off was that these copies were non-returnable; the store bought the inventory, and if any didn't sell, the store was stuck with it. This arrangement benefited publishers, who could now advertise a comic book in advance through a direct market catalogue, get their sales figures back, and then print only the amount that stores ordered. (The downside for publishers, however, was that stores ordered fewer copies, cautious not to get saddled with a lot of leftover unsold stock.) For comic book creators like Wendy and Richard Pini, the direct market meant a better chance of cultivating a readership to come back to their comic issue after issue, which gave them the freedom to tell longer, more involved stories. The direct market is exactly what made comics like *Elfquest* possible.

After the initial 20-issue run at WaRP, Marvel licensed *Elfquest* from the Pinis and reprinted the original series starting in 1985. The Marvel Comics format of 22 pages was shorter than the magazine-sized issues of the initial run, so the publisher expanded the series to 32 issues, commissioning all-new pages to accommodate the new pacing. Needless to say, this brought *Elfquest* to a much wider audience and grew its fan base. Meanwhile, Wendy and Richard continued to publish new *Elfquest* issues through WaRP for more than 15 years.

In 2003, DC Comics contracted with the Pinis to take up the publishing of *Elfquest*, releasing new installments as one-shots and miniseries, as well as reprinting the original series. By the mid-2000s, such sprawling amounts of the Elfquest saga had been published that the Pinis sought out new methods of making it accessible to new readers; they began posting the entire series on the Elfquest website.

The Pinis made a new publishing deal with Dark Horse Comics in 2012, and in 2013, the publisher released the one-shot *Elfquest Special: The Final Quest*, followed by a *Final Quest* series that ran for five years and 24 issues. Wendy and Richard Pini finally brought the saga of Cutter and the elves of  the World of Two Moons to a close with the publication of the final issue on February 28, 2018—exactly 40 years to the day since the debut of *Elfquest*.

GLOSSARY

ALBUM: A softcover or hardbound volume of comics, usually between 60 and 100 pages, containing a single story, a collection of serial chapters, or an installment of a series. Primarily a European format, where albums are more common than floppy comic books or graphic novels.

CARTOONIST: Although it might refer specifically to a creator of humorous newspaper strips or editorial cartoons satirizing current events, "cartoonist" is a common term for any creator who writes and draws their own work, as opposed to a collaboration between writer and artist.

COMIC BOOK: A floppy magazine of comics, most commonly bound with staples, usually featuring a short installment centered around a character or theme, or a serial chapter of an ongoing narrative.

COMICS: The most common name used for the medium of stories told via drawings in sequence, with panels simulating the passage of narrative time, with or without text for dialogue and narration.

COMIC STRIP: A short installment of comics printed in a newspaper or magazine, usually a single page or just a few panels, though sometimes as long as a few pages. When posted online, strips are sometimes referred to as webcomics.

GRAPHIC NOVEL: A softcover or hardcover bound volume of comics, designed to live on a bookshelf with the title printed on the spine. Usually consists of a single, book-length story, or an installment of an ongoing series of book-length volumes.

MANGA: The specific format of comics in Japan, frequently in black and white, usually serialized in a magazine and collected in multiple volumes of small books.

PEN NAME: Also called a pseudonym; a name assumed by creators, either to hide their identity or simply because it sounds catchy; Stanley Lieber became Stan Lee, Jacob Kurtzberg became Jack Kirby, and Georges Remi became Hergé, among others.

PULP: At the peak of publishing entertainment in the 1930s and '40s, novels and magazines printed on cheap, pulpy paper told thrilling stories of fantastic adventure, science fiction, fantasy, crime, and horror and were an early inspiration to comic book creators. "Pulp" came to refer to these books and magazines, and to the kinds of stories in them.

SUPERHERO: A character with special powers beyond human ability, frequently with a secret identity; also the genre of superhero comics long dominant in American comic book publishing.

INDEX

CITATIONS

Page 42: "The first story is nothing great…" *Lee, Stan, Letter to the Comic Reader* #16, self-published fan magazine. February 1963.

Page 57: "Oh, Stan, do you have a few minutes?" Steinberg, Flo and Stan Lee, *Voices of Marvel*, track 1, 1965.

Page 65: "Yes, he has a costume!" Eisner, Will, *The Jack Kirby Collector* #16, TwoMorrows Publishing. July 1997. Archived at http://www.twomorrows.com/kirby/articles/16eisner.html, accessed April 26, 2019.

AWESOME MINDS

Comic Book Creators

MORE BOOKS ABOUT CREATING COMICS

Beauchamp, Monte. *Masterful Marks: Cartoonists Who Changed the World*. New York, NY: Simon & Schuster, 2014.

Bell, Blake. *Strange and Stranger: The World of Steve Ditko*. Seattle, WA: Fantagraphics Books, 2008.

Eisner, Will. *Comics and Sequential Art: Principles & Practices from the Legendary Cartoonist*. New York, NY: W.W. Norton & Company, 2008.

Evanier, Mark. *Kirby: King of Comics*. New York, NY: Abrams, 2008.

Lee, Stan, and John Buscema. *How to Draw Comics the Marvel Way*. New York, NY: Simon & Schuster, 1984.

McCloud, Scott. *Understanding Comics: The Invisible Art*. New York, NY: HarperCollins, 1994.

Telgemeier, *Raina. Share Your Smile: Raina's Guide to Telling Your Own Story*. New York, NY: Scholastic, 2019.

Van Lente, Fred, and Ryan Dunlavey. *The Comic Book History of Comics: Birth of a Medium*. San Diego, CA: IDW Publishing, 2017.